MARY MACLANE

THE STORY OF MARY MACLANE & *Other Writings*

with texts by
Henry B. Fuller, Clarence Darrow
& Harriet Monroe

Edited & Introduced by
Penelope Rosemont

Chicago
CHARLES H. KERR PUBLISHING COMPANY
1997

This collection of writings by
Mary MacLane
is dedicated to my
Aunt Millie,
one of the family's
great iconoclasts.
—P.R.

ACKNOWLEDGEMENTS

Many friends and an even larger number of strangers helped in the preparation of this book. I especially want to thank Diana Haskell and others in Special Collections, The Newberry Library, Chicago (which houses an important collection of Mary MacLane materials), and the helpful staffs of the Butte-Silver Bow Public Library, Butte, Montana; the Montana Historical Society, Helena; the Chicago Historical Society; Northwestern University in Evanston; and the New York Public Library.

Thanks also to Paul Garon, Erin Gibson, Justin O'Brien, Constance Rosemont, and Franklin Rosemont for technical and other assistance.

A shorter version of the Introduction appeared in *Free Spirits: Annals of the Insurgent Imagination* (City Lights Books, 1983).

P.R.

ISBN 0-88286-233-2 (paper)
First Edition

Printed on recycled paper.

Write for our complete catalog.

Charles H. Kerr Publishing Company
1740 West Greenleaf Avenue
Chicago, Illinois 60626

WHAT THE CRITICS HAVE SAID ABOUT
MARY MACLANE

"An extraordinary book. . . . The boldest will consider it daring; even those who are far from being prudes may find it shocking. . . . Mary MacLane is a genius. . . . Her ideas are all her own. Nobody could be more decidedly a repository of originality."

—Henry Blake Fuller in the *Chicago American* (1902)

"It is only charity to say that Mary MacLane is mad. . . . She should be put under medical treatment, and pens and paper kept out of her way until she is restored to reason."

—*New York Herald* (1902)

"Readers have laughed over her ravings, with now and then a feeling of disgust that they find pleasure in anything so depraved, so low, so utterly worthless."

—*Great Falls Daily Tribune* (1902)

"A feminine Rousseau—only more frank. . . . A remarkable human document, the strangest book printed in years."

—*Washington Post* (1902)

"She has voiced the protests of thousands of women against conventionality . . . but she has marred much that is true by low cunning and vulgarity. . . . She will be criticized, condemned and ridiculed, and she will deserve all censure given."

—*The Missoulian* (1902)

"I do not hesitate to say that I admire the lady, let the chips fall where they may. She's one of the few damsels in this republic . . . who actually knows how to write English. . . . She senses the infinite resilience, the drunken exuberance, the magnificent power and delicacy of the language."

—H. L. Mencken (1917)

"This errant daughter of literature . . . represented the missing link between the shaved bare leg of the present and the bashful ankle of the past. . . . The career of Mary MacLane is Chapter I in *The History of Flapperism.*"

—*The Chicagoan* (1929)

"The restless, discontented, 'New Woman' would later become a literary cliché, but in 1902 Mary MacLane's confessions were the first such expression of this important phase in the feminist movement."

—Carolyn J. Mattern (1977)

Charles H. Kerr Established 1886

Mary MacLane
Frontispiece of the first edition of *The Story of Mary MacLane*
(Chicago, 1902)

TABLE OF CONTENTS

MARVELOUS MARY MACLANE

"I of womankind and of nineteen years, will now begin to set down as full and frank a Portrayal as I am able of myself, Mary MacLane, for whom the world contains not a parallel." Thus begins one of the most unusual books in our literature, by one of the most scandalous American writers.

When *The Story of Mary MacLane* was published by the prestigious Chicago firm of Herbert S. Stone and Company in April 1902, its author was skyrocketed to nationwide notoriety. The book was an immediate sensation. Nothing like it had ever been seen before, and the fact that it was the work of a teen-age girl—living in Butte, Montana, of all places—made the scandal complete. Every Associated Press affiliate in the country ran a front-page story on it. Here for the first time was a young woman's "inner life shown in its nakedness":

> *I have discovered for myself the art that lies in obscure shadows. I have discovered the art of the day of small things . . . I care neither for right nor for wrong—my conscience is nil. My brain is a conglomeration of aggressive versatility. I have reached a truly wonderful state of miserable morbid unhappiness . . . May I never become that abnormal, merciless animal, that deformed monstrosity—a virtuous woman . . . .*

Respectable critics roared their disapproval. "Mary MacLane is mad," wrote the *New York Herald*. "She should be put under medical treatment, and pens and paper kept out of her way until she is restored to reason." The *New York Times* urged that she be spanked. Other critics raised the charge of "obscenity." When the Butte Public Library announced that it would not allow the book on its shelves, the *Helena Daily Independent* applauded, arguing that if this book "should go in, all the self-respecting books in the library would jump out of the window."

The Story of Mary MacLane was an instant bestseller. 80,000 copies were sold the first month alone, and the resulting $17,000 in royalties allowed MacLane to fulfill her greatest ambition: to escape Butte. The book went through several printings, and its author remained front-page news for years. Mary MacLane Societies were organized by young women all over the country. The popular vaudeville team of Weber and Fields—remembered today mostly as the introducers of pie-in-the-face gags—did a burlesque of the book. A full-length spoof was published, titled *The Story of Willie Complain.* "Montana's lit'ry lady" found her way into the comics and popular songs. There was even a Mary MacLane Highball, "with or without ice-cream, cooling, refreshing, invigorating, devilish, the up-to-date drink."

The rage for "MacLaneism," against which leading critics from coast to coast declaimed so fervently, also had its more somber aspect. It was reported that a Chicago girl who had organized the local Mary MacLane Society was arrested for stealing a horse. She said she committed the theft because she needed the experience for a novel she was writing. And on 4 May 1902 the *Great Falls Daily Tribune* told of a Michigan 15-year-old who "imagined herself ill-used and misunderstood. The reading of the morbid ravings of the Butte girl convinced her that she was, and a dose of arsenic followed. She died with a copy of the book in her hands." According to some reports, MacLane's book prompted a whole rash of suicides.

Who *was* Mary MacLane—this Montana girl who drove literary critics to distraction and made moralists furious, and whose book was said to provoke insanity, crime and suicide?

Descended from "a long line of Scotch and Canadian MacLanes," Mary was born in Winnipeg, Manitoba, on 2 May 1881. Throughout her life she was fiercely proud of her father's "Highland Scot" heritage, and she considered her own rebellious genius to be a direct result of it. At age four her family moved to western Minnesota. Her father died when she was eight. A few years later, after her mother had remarried—this time to "a mining man"—they pressed on to Montana, finally settling in Butte in the mid-1890s. Those who knew Mary MacLane in those years recalled her as a studious, withdrawn and somewhat morbid child; her schoolmates called her "The Centerville Ghost" because she liked to prowl around the local cemetery at night. For two years she edited the Butte High School paper. She graduated in 1899, with proficiency in Latin, Greek and other languages.

She seems to have read whatever came her way—everything from Nick Carter pulp mysteries to Confucius to *Foxe's Book of Martyrs.* Drawn to the great Romantic poets, Byron and Keats above all, she was also fond of "books for boys." She did not, however, care for "girls' books": "I felt as if I had more in common with the Jews wandering through the wilderness, or with a band of fighting Amazons."

Well-versed in the history of the struggle for women's rights, she read and liked the feminist authors—especially Susan B. Anthony, Elizabeth Cady Stanton, and Victoria Woodhull—but took no part in the organized women's movement. Similarly, she admired "the noise and color and morale of the crowds on a Miners' Union Day" (Butte was a stronghold of the militant Western Federation of Miners, and later of the Industrial Workers of the World), but remained outside the ranks of organized labor. "I am always alone," she wrote. "I might mingle with people intimately every hour of my life, still I should be alone."

Outwardly her life remained in many ways as severely restricted as that of most women in the turn-of-the-century United States, crushed beneath the weight of custom and crippled by prejudice. But inwardly her spirit yearned for love, adventure and the marvelous, and teemed with a defiance that found expression in her writing. It was what she did with these yearnings and this defiance that makes her work so unique and important. And what did she do? Simply, brilliantly, rigorously, she revealed the real working of her mind in the various circumscribed situations of daily life.

"The clearest lights on persons," she noted, "are small salient personal facts and items about them and their ways of life." Out of these "small salient personal facts" Mary MacLane elaborated her own myth—a myth of herself. From the seemingly most trivial things that surrounded her, she distilled a pure magic. She wrote, with sensuous detail, on "the art of eating an olive," on her long walks over Butte's endless "sand and barrenness," on the sexual longings stirred in her by seventeen engraved portraits of Napoleon. Narcissistically, obsessively, playfully, she explored the infinite irrational depths of her recalcitrant subjectivity. "Just to be Mary MacLane—who am first of all my own self, and get by with it!—how I do that I cannot quite make out."

After *The Story of Mary MacLane* she published two more books: *My Friend Annabel Lee* (1903) and *I, Mary MacLane* (1917). She also contributed feature articles to a number of newspapers and magazines. None of her writings fit into the usual literary classifications. They are neither fiction nor non-fiction; they are not "stream-of-consciousness" narratives and should not be confused with "true confessions." Although presented in diary form, they are really something quite different. They are certainly not autobiography, philosophy or psychology, any more than they are stories, essays or poems. Mary MacLane defied existing genres and created her own.

Poetic humor is her hallmark. Much of her work, such as "The Six Toothbrushes" and "The Back of a Magazine," makes us think of Lautréamont and Jarry. There is an "anti-literary" quality about her writing—anti-literary in the sense intended by André Breton and Paul Eluard when they declared that "poetry is the opposite of literature." Although an avid reader she disdained the society of *littérateurs,* and contributed rarely, if at all, to literary reviews. Her eccentric, playful yet radical divergence from the dominant literary tendencies of her time qualify her as an authentic presurrealist.

"I do not write what my thoughts are saying to me," she acknowledged, although "now and again I think I catch some truth by the sweat of its Rhythm." But "something lives, lives muscularly in me that constantly betrays me, destroys me against all my own convictions, against all my own knowledge, against all my own desire." With the same striking candor she recognized the limits of her own self-assigned project: "It is as if I have made a portrait not of Me, but of a Room I have just quitted."

If most critics disparaged her with uncomprehending malice, there were at least a few exceptions. Novelist Gertrude Atherton, who visited her and wrote about her at length, admired not only her writing but also her conversation, "a mixture of slang and prose of an almost classical purity"; she found, too, that MacLane's "criticisms of current authors were acute, unbiased, and everything she said was worth listening to." Hamlin Garland praised "her crisp, clear, unhesitating use of English." H. L.

Mencken admired her sense of "the infinite resilience, the drunken exuberance, the magnificent power and delicacy of the language," and said he knew of no other woman writer who could play on words more magically. In a full-page review in the *Chicago American* Clarence Darrow pronounced *The Story of Mary MacLane* "little short of a miracle," and went on to say that "No more marvelous book was ever born of a sensitive, precocious brain." Socialist Oscar Lovell Triggs saluted MacLane's courage in portraying "the inner history of her life." And Harriet Monroe, who went on to become founding editor of *Poetry* magazine, likened her to Emily Brontë and elsewhere stated that she had never met anyone with more analytical power.

After *The Story of Mary MacLane* was published, the young author visited Chicago and then went East for a time. Rumor had it that she might enroll in Radcliffe College or Vassar, but nothing came of it. She found life in Boston and Cambridge dull compared to Butte, "where the people are so much more virile and full of imagination." She much preferred New York, especially Greenwich Village, where she kept an apartment for several years. Her New York writings include an affectionate sketch of Coney Island and a strong indictment of Wall Street.

Wherever she went she was sure to confound the philistines with her unconventional behavior. She went out of her way to insult Butte society matrons who staged a literary reception in her honor. A trip to Newport, Rhode Island provoked an article sharply critical of that fashionable resort-town's class pretensions and arrogance. Mary MacLane simply could not be "domesticated." Violating social conventions was the essence of her being. At a time when tolerance of dissident sexuality was virtually non-existent, she openly avowed her Lesbian inclinations. We find her refereeing a prizefight in Thermopolis, Wyoming, and frequenting low-class gambling dives on 42nd Street in New York. In later years she seems to have rejected literary society altogether and, with characteristic defiance of white middle-class propriety, chose to live instead in Chicago's African American community. Always, everywhere, she freely expounded her controversial views on marriage, the family, sex, religion, literature, morality, the greed and idiocy of the rich, and anything else that came to mind.

Unlike so many authors who enjoy initial success in Chicago and then move to New York to grow old and respectable, in 1917 Mary MacLane came back to the city of her youthful triumph for what turned out to be a second triumph, of sorts—or at least another scandal in the grand MacLane tradition: She made a movie! An "ardent film fan" herself, when she received an invitation to make a film from producer George K. Spohr of Chicago's renowned Essanay studios, where Charlie Chaplin made his greatest shorts, she readily accepted. Shortly after her arrival in town, production began on the full-length feature, *Men Who Have Made Love to Me*. Not only did MacLane write the script—based on an article of the same title she had published in 1910—she also played the starring role: herself.

Directed by Arthur Berthelet, the seven- or eight-reel "Men Who. . ." was released in January 1918, and was widely reviewed throughout the country. Unfortunately, no print of this film appears to have survived. Most critics didn't care for it, needless to say, although a few begrudged her some ability as an actress, and her director said that the comic vamp reminded him of the young Sarah Bernhardt. Not surprisingly, the film provoked the wrath of puritanical Public Opinion; it was banned by the Ohio Board of Censors as "harmful to public morality."

And so Mary MacLane, who embodied much of the spirit of the "Jazz Age" two decades early, was still going strong in 1918. Not for nothing has she been called the earliest example of the "New Woman" in literature, and even "the first flapper." But when the Roaring Twenties roared into full swing, she was no longer the constant headliner she had been in her youth. After the furor provoked by her movie died down, she settled in Chicago. Her contract with Essanay called for a series of films, but she made no others. In part this may have been because the first film was not a box-office hit, but MacLane's failing health was surely another and perhaps greater factor. She had been considered frail even as a child, and in 1910 she suffered a severe case of scarlet fever. Sometime in the 1920s, if not earlier, she was diagnosed as having tuberculosis.

She was cared for during her last years by her best friend, the African American photographer and longtime Chicagoan Harriet Williams, whom she had met through New York acquaintances not long after her first book came out in 1902. The two had stayed in touch and were especially close during MacLane's last four years. On 6 August 1929, she died in her room at the Michigan Hotel on South Michigan Avenue, not far from Williams' studio. She was forty-eight years old. Williams, together with Harriet Monroe, arranged her funeral.

For decades after her death Mary MacLane remained largely an unknown. Her books were long out of print and difficult to find, even in libraries. Standard literary histories and anthologies ignored her completely, and until recently even feminist writers rarely referred to her except in passing. Amazingly, she is not profiled in the three-volume reference work, *Notable American Women.*

Yet MacLane's is an important voice, rebellious and original, and surely will be listened to again. At a time when most U.S. "women's literature" reeked of genteel sentimentality, moralistic uplift, and other literary sugar-water, she offered readers stronger stuff by far. Scandalously, passionately, she rejected bourgeois-christian notions of "femininity" and scorned the patriotic platitudes about life in the U.S.A. Above all she affirmed her right to a free sexuality, and insisted that the quest for experience and self-realization is too important to allow it to be impeded by stupid, narrow-minded bigots and bureaucrats. After nearly a hundred years, her radical pessimism, her individualist feminism, her refusal to adjust to the the misery and hypocrisy of an unjust and exploitative social order have retained and even multiplied their force, and more than ever win our respect and admiration.

"I can shake my life like a hollow gourd," said Mary MacLane, "and hear the eerie rattling sound I make in it." There is a bitter humor in these words, as in so much of her writing. Although she felt that her humor was "far too deep to admit of laughter," she coolly and calmly insisted on keeping the last laugh for herself. "In my black dress and my still room, I say inwardly and willy-nilly, and with all my Heart and relishingly: Ha! ha! ha!"

Penelope Rosemont

Chicago, June 1997

A NOTE ON THE TEXT

The Story of Mary MacLane follows the text of the original Herbert S. Stone edition of 1902, except that I have corrected two typographical errors after consulting the author's original manuscript in The Newberry Library in Chicago. It is a tribute to MacLane's ability as a writer, as well as to the intelligence of her publisher, that the book appeared with unusually light editing. The few changes consisted almost entirely of minor details of punctuation (removing, for example, MacLane's archaic dashes after periods at the ends of paragraphs), and thus do not in the least affect the author's meaning.

MacLane's publisher did make one really significant change, and surely for the better. MacLane had titled her book *I Await the Devil's Coming*, but the publisher brought it out as *The Story of Mary MacLane*, unfortunately without notifying the author of the change. In a letter dated 22 April 1902 (in the Newberry Library collection), MacLane said she did "not fancy" the new title, but went on to dismiss her complaint as a "trivial matter," and readily deferred to the publisher's judgement.

The excerpts from *My Friend Annabel Lee* (1903) and *I, Mary MacLane* (1917) also follow the text of their first published editions. A few of these appeared, slightly abridged, in my mini-Mary-MacLane anthology in *Free Spirits: Annals of the Insurgent Imagination* in 1983; the others are reprinted here for the first time, as are MacLane's articles, with the exception of "A Day in Wall Street."

To the best of my knowledge, the texts on MacLane by Clarence Darrow, Henry Blake Fuller, Harriet Monroe, and the anonymous editor of *The Chicagoan* have not previously been reprinted. In Darrow's article I have omitted his many long quotations from MacLane's book. The others are reprinted in full.

In the few cases where I have changed titles, I have noted the original title at the end of the text, together with the source and date of first publication.

P.R.

THE STORY OF MARY MACLANE

BUTTE, MONTANA,
13 JANUARY 1901.

I OF womankind and of nineteen years, will now begin to set down as full and frank a Portrayal as I am able of myself, Mary MacLane, for whom the world contains not a parallel.

I am convinced of this, for I am odd.

I am distinctly original innately and in development.

I have in me a quite unusual intensity of life.

I can feel.

I have a marvelous capacity for misery and for happiness.

I am broad-minded.

I am a genius.

I am a philosopher of my own good peripatetic school.

I care neither for right nor for wrong—my conscience is nil.

My brain is a conglomeration of aggressive versatility.

I have reached a truly wonderful state of miserable morbid unhappiness.

I know myself, oh, very well.

I have attained an egotism that is rare indeed.

I have gone into the deep shadows.

All this constitutes oddity. I find, therefore, that I am quite, quite odd.

I have hunted for even the suggestion of a parallel among the several hundred persons that I call acquaintances. But in vain. There are people and people of varying depths and intricacies of character, but there is none to compare with me. The young ones of my own age—if I chance to give them but a glimpse of the real workings of my mind—can only stare at me in dazed stupidity, uncomprehending; and the old ones of forty and fifty—for forty and fifty are always old to nineteen—can but either stare also in stupidity, or else, their own narrowness asserting itself, smile their little devilish smile of superiority which they reserve indiscriminately for all foolish young things. The utter idiocy of forty and fifty at times!

These, to be sure, are extreme instances. There are among my young acquaintances some who do not stare in stupidity, and yes, even at forty and fifty there are some who understand some phases of my complicated character, though none to comprehend it in its entirety.

But, as I said, even the suggestion of a parallel is not to be found among them.

I think at this moment, however, of two minds famous in the world of letters between which and mine there are certain fine points of similarity. These are the minds of Lord Byron and of Marie Bashkirtseff. It is the Byron of "Don Juan" in whom I find suggestions of myself. In this sublime outpouring there are few to admire the character of Don Juan, but all must admire Byron. He is truly admirable. He uncovered and exposed his soul of mingled good and bad—as the terms are—for the world to gaze upon. He knew the human race, and he knew himself.

As for that strange notable, Marie Bashkirtseff, yes, I am rather like her in many points, as I've been told. But in most things I go beyond her.

Where she is deep, I am deeper.

Where she is wonderful in her intensity, I am still more wonderful in my intensity.

Where she had philosophy, I am a philosopher.

Where she had astonishing vanity and conceit, I have yet more astonishing vanity and conceit.

But she, forsooth, could paint good pictures,—and I—what can I do?

She had a beautiful face, and I am a plain-featured, insignificant little animal.

She was surrounded by admiring, sympathetic friends, and I am alone—alone, though there are people and people.

She was a genius, and still more am I a genius.

She suffered with the pain of a woman, young; and I suffer with the pain of a woman, young and all alone.

And so it is.

Along some lines I have gotten to the edge of the world. A step more and I fall off. I do not take the step. I stand on the edge, and I suffer.

Nothing, oh, nothing on the earth can suffer like a woman

young and all alone!

—Before proceeding farther with the Portraying of Mary MacLane, I will write out some of her uninteresting history.

I was born in 1881 at Winnipeg, in Canada. Whether Winnipeg will yet live to be proud of this fact is a matter for some conjecture and anxiety on my part. When I was four years old I was taken with my family to a little town in western Minnesota, where I lived a more or less vapid and lonely life until I was ten. We came then to Montana.

Whereat the aforesaid life was continued.

My father died when I was eight.

Apart from feeding and clothing me comfortably and sending me to school—which is no more than was due me—and transmitting to me the MacLane blood and character, I can not see that he ever gave me a single thought.

Certainly he did not love me, for he was quite incapable of loving any one but himself. And since nothing is of any moment in this world without the love of human beings for each other, it is a matter of supreme indifference to me whether my father, Jim MacLane of selfish memory, lived or died.

He is nothing to me.

There are with me still a mother, a sister, and two brothers.

They also are nothing to me.

They do not understand me any more than if I were some strange live curiosity, as which I dare say they regard me.

I am peculiarly of the MacLane blood, which is Highland Scotch. My sister and brothers inherit the traits of their mother's family, which is of Scotch Lowland descent. This alone makes no small degree of difference. Apart from this the MacLanes—these particular MacLanes—are just a little bit different from every family in Canada, and from every other that I've known. It contains and has contained fanatics of many minds—religious, social, whatnot, and I am a true MacLane.

There is absolutely no sympathy between my immediate family and me. There can never be. My mother, having been with me during the whole of my nineteen years, has an utterly distorted idea of my nature and its desires, if indeed she has any idea of it.

When I think of the exquisite love and sympathy which might be between a mother and daughter, I feel myself defrauded of a beautiful thing rightfully mine, in a world where for me such things are pitiably few.

It will always be so.

My sister and brothers are not interested in me and my analyses and philosophy, and my wants. Their own are strictly practical and material. The love and sympathy between human beings is to them, it seems, a thing only for people in books.

In short, they are Lowland Scotch, and I am a MacLane.

And so, as I've said, I carried my uninteresting existence into Montana. The existence became less uninteresting, however, as my versatile mind began to develop and grow and know the glittering things that are. But I realized as the years were passing that my own life was at best a vapid, negative thing.

A thousand treasures that I wanted were lacking.

I graduated from the high school with these things: very good Latin; good French and Greek; indifferent geometry and other mathematics; a broad conception of history and literature; peripatetic philosophy that I acquired without any aid from the High school; genius of a kind, that has always been with me; an empty heart that has taken on a certain wooden quality; an excellent strong young woman's-body; a pitiably starved soul.

With this equipment I have gone my way through the last two years. But my life, though unsatisfying and warped, is no longer insipid. It is fraught with a poignant misery—the misery of nothingness.

I have no particular thing to occupy me. I write every day. Writing is a necessity—like eating. I do a little housework, and on the whole I am rather fond of it—some parts of it. I dislike dusting chairs, but I have no aversion to scrubbing floors. Indeed, I have gained much of my strength and gracefulness of body from scrubbing the kitchen floor—to say nothing of some fine points of philosophy. It brings a certain energy to one's body and to one's brain.

But mostly I take walks far away in the open country. Butte and its immediate vicinity present as ugly an outlook as one could wish to see. It is so ugly indeed that it is near the perfection of ugliness. And anything perfect, or nearly so, is not to be despised. I have reached some astonishing subtleties of conception as I have walked for miles over the sand and barrenness among the little hills and gulches. Their utter desolateness is an inspiration to the long, long thoughts and to the nameless wanting. Every day I walk over the sand and barrenness.

And so, then, my daily life seems an ordinary life enough, and possibly, to an ordinary person, a comfortable life.

That's as may be.

To me it is an empty, damned weariness.

I rise in the morning; eat three meals; and walk; and work a little, read a little, write; see some uninteresting people; go to bed.

Next day, I rise in the morning; eat three meals; and walk; and work a little, read a little, write; see some uninteresting people; go to bed.

Again I rise in the morning; eat three meals; and walk; and work a little, read a little, write; see some uninteresting people; go to bed.

Truly an exalted, soulful life!

What it does for me, how it affects me, I am now trying to portray.

14 JANUARY.

I HAVE in me the germs of intense life. If I could *live*, and if I could succeed in writing out my living, the world itself would feel the heavy intensity of it.

I have the personality, the nature, of a Napoleon, albeit a feminine translation. And therefore I do not conquer; I do not even fight. I manage only to exist.

Poor little Mary MacLane!—what might you not be? What wonderful things might you not do? But held down, half-buried, a seed fallen in barren ground, alone, uncomprehended, obscure—poor little Mary MacLane! Weep, world,—why don't you?—for poor little Mary MacLane!

Had I been born a man I would by now have made a deep impression of myself on the world—on some part of it. But I am a woman, and God, or the Devil, or Fate, or whosoever it was, has flayed me of the thick outer skin and thrown me out into the midst of life—has left me a lonely, damned thing filled with the red, red blood of ambition and desire, but afraid to be touched, for there is no thick skin between my sensitive flesh and the world's fingers.

But I want to be touched.

Napoleon was a man, and though sensitive his flesh was safely covered.

But I am a woman, awakening, and upon awakening and looking about me, I would fain turn and go back to sleep.

There is a pain that goes with these things when one is a woman, young, and all alone.

I am filled with an ambition. I wish to give to the world a naked Portrayal of Mary MacLane: her wooden heart, her good young woman's-body, her mind, her soul.

I wish to write, write, write!

I wish to acquire that beautiful, benign, gentle, satisfying thing—Fame. I want it—oh, I want it! I wish to leave all my obscurity, my misery—my weary unhappiness—behind me forever.

I am deadly, deadly tired of my unhappiness.

I wish this Portrayal to be published and launched into that deep salt sea—the world. There are some there surely who will understand it and me.

Can I be that thing, which I am—can I be possessed of a peculiar rare genius, and yet drag out my life in obscurity in this uncouth, warped, Montana town?

It must be impossible! If I thought the world contained nothing more than that for me—oh, what should I do? Would I make an end of my dreary little life now? I fear I would. I am a philosopher—and a coward. And it were infinitely better to die now in the high-beating pulses of youth than to drag on, year after year, year after year, and find oneself at last a stagnant old woman, spiritless, hopeless, with a declining body, a declining mind,—and nothing to look back upon except the visions of things that might have been—and the weariness.

I see the picture. I see it plainly. Oh, kind Devil, deliver me from it!

Surely there must be in a world of manifold beautiful things something among them for me. And always, while I am still young, there is that dim light, the Future. But it is indeed a dim, dim light, and ofttimes there's a treachery in it.

15 JANUARY.

SO THEN, yes. I find myself at this stage of womankind and nineteen years, a genius, a thief, a liar—a general moral vagabond, a fool more or less, and a philosopher of the peripatetic school. Also I find that even this combination can not make one happy. It serves, however, to occupy my versatile mind, to keep me wondering what it is a kind Devil has in store for me.

A philosopher of my own peripatetic school—hour after hour I walk over the desolate sand and dreariness among tiny hills and gulches on the outskirts of this mining town; in the morning, in the long afternoon, in the cool of the night. And hour after hour, as I walk, through my brain some long, long pageants march: the pageant of my fancies, the pageant of my unparalleled egotism, the pageant of my unhappiness, the pageant of my minute analyzing, the pageant of my peculiar philosophy, the pageant of my dull, dull life,—and the pageant of the Possibilities.

We three go out on the sand and barrenness: my wooden heart, my good young woman's-body, my soul. We go there and contemplate the long sandy wastes, the red, red line on the sky at the setting of the sun, the cold gloomy mountains under it, the ground without a weed, without a grass-blade even in their season—for they have years ago been killed off by the sulphur smoke from the smelters.

So this sand and barrenness forms the setting for the personality of me.

16 JANUARY.

I FEEL about forty years old.

Yet I know my feeling is not the feeling of forty years. These are the feelings of miserable, wretched youth.

Every day the atmosphere of a house becomes unbearable, so every day I go out to the sand and barrenness. It is not cold, neither is it mild. It is gloomy.

I sit for two hours on the ground by the side of a pitiably

small narrow stream of water. It is not even a natural stream. I dare say it comes from some mine among the hills. But it is well enough that the stream is not natural—when you consider the sand and barrenness. It is singularly appropriate.

And I am singularly appropriate to all of them. It is good, after all, to be appropriate to something—to be in touch with something, even sand and barrenness. The sand and barrenness is old—oh, very old. You think of this when you look at it.

What should I do if the earth were made of wood, with a paper sky!

I feel about forty years old.

And again I say I know my feeling is not the feeling of forty years. These are the feelings of miserable, wretched youth.

Still more pitiable than the sand and barrenness and the poor unnatural stream is the dry, warped cemetery where the dry, warped people of Butte bury their dead friends. It is a source of satisfaction to me to walk down to this cemetery and contemplate it, and revel in its utter pitiableness.

"It is more pitiable than I and my sand and barrenness and my poor unnatural stream," I say over and over, and take my comfort.

Its condition is more forlorn than that of a woman young and alone. It is unkempt. It is choked with dust and stones. The few scattered blades of grass look rather ashamed to be seen growing there. A great many of the headstones are of wood and are in a shameful state of decay. Those that are of stone are still more shameful in their hard brightness.

The dry, warped friends of the dry, warped people of Butte are buried in this dusty, dreary, wind-havocked waste. They are left here and forgotten.

The Devil must rejoice in this graveyard.

And I rejoice with the Devil.

It is something for me to contemplate that is more pitiable than I and my sand and barrenness and my unnatural stream.

I rejoice with the Devil.

The inhabitants of this cemetery are forgotten. I have watched once the burying of a young child. Every day for a fortnight afterward I came back, and I saw the mother of the child there. She came and stood by the small new grave. After a few days more she stopped coming.

I knew the woman and went to her house to see her. She was beginning to forget the child. She was beginning to take up again the thread of her life where she had let it go. The thread of her life is involved in the divorces and fights of her neighbors.

Out in the warped graveyard her child is forgotten. And presently the wooden headstone will begin to decay. But the worms will not forget their part. They have eaten the small body by now, and enjoyed it. Always worms enjoy a body to eat.

And also the Devil rejoiced.

And I rejoiced with the Devil.

They are more pitiable, I insist, than I and my sand and barrenness—the mother whose life is involved in divorces and fights, and the worms eating at the child's body, and the wooden headstone which will presently decay.

And so the Devil and I rejoice.

But no matter how ferociously pitiable is the dried-up graveyard, the sand and barrenness and the sluggish little stream have their own persistent individual damnation. The world is at least so constructed that its treasures may be damned each in a different manner and degree.

I feel about forty years old.

And I know my feeling is not the feeling of forty years. They do not feel any of these things at forty. At forty the fire has long since burned out. When I am forty I shall look back to myself and my feelings at nineteen and I shall smile.

Or shall I indeed smile?

17 JANUARY.

AS I have said, I want Fame. I want to write—to write such things as compel the admiring acclamations of the world at large; such things as are written but once in years, things subtly but distinctly different from the books written every day.

I can do this.

Let me but make a beginning, let me but strike the world in a vulnerable spot, and I can take it by storm. Let me but win my spurs, and then you will see me—of womankind and young, valiantly astride a charger riding down the world, with Fame following at the charger's heels, and the multitudes agape.

But oh, more than all this I want to be happy!

Fame is indeed benign and gentle and satisfying. But Happiness is something at once tender and brilliant beyond all things.

I want Fame more than I can tell.

But more than I want Fame I want Happiness. I have never been happy in my weary young life.

Think, oh, *think*, of being happy for a year—for a day! How brilliantly blue the sky would be; how swiftly and joyously would the green rivers run; how madly, merrily triumphant the four winds of heaven would sweep round the corners of the fair earth!

What would I not give for one day, one hour, of that charmed thing Happiness! What would I not give up?

How we eager fools tread on each other's heels, and tear each other's hair, and scratch each other's faces, in our furious gallop after Happiness! For some it is embodied in Fame, for some in Money, for some in Power, for some in Virtue—and for me in something very much like love.

None of the other fools desires Happiness as I desire it. For one single hour of Happiness I would give up at once these things: Fame, and Money, and Power, and Virtue, and Honor, and Righteousness, and Truth, and Logic, and Philosophy, and Genius. The while I would say, What a little, little price to pay for dear Happiness!

I am ready and waiting to give all that I have to the Devil in exchange for Happiness. I have been tortured so long with the dull, dull misery of Nothingness—all my nineteen years. I want to be happy—oh, I want to be happy!

The Devil has not yet come. But I know that he usually comes, and I wait him eagerly.

I am fortunate that I am not one of those who are burdened with an innate sense of virtue and honor which must come always before Happiness. They are but few who find their Happiness in their Virtue. The rest of them must be content to see it walk away.

But with me Virtue and Honor are nothing.
I long unspeakably for Happiness.
And so I await the Devil's coming.

18 JANUARY.

AND meanwhile—as I wait—my mind occupies itself with its own good odd philosophy, so that even the Nothingness becomes almost endurable.

The Devil has given me some good things—for I find that the Devil owns and rules the earth and all that therein is. He has given me, among other things—my admirable young woman's-body, which I enjoy thoroughly and of which I am passionately fond.

A spasm of pleasure seizes me when I think in some acute moment of the buoyant health and vitality of this fine young body that is feminine in every fiber.

You may gaze at and admire the picture in the front of this book. It is the picture of a genius—a genius with a good strong young woman's-body,—and inside the pictured body is a liver, a MacLane liver, of admirable perfectness.

Other young women and older women and men of all ages have good bodies also, I doubt not—though the masculine body is merely flesh, it seems, flesh and bones and nothing else. But few recognize the value of their bodies; few have grasped the possibilities, the artistic graceful perfection, the poetry of human flesh in its health. Few have even sense enough indeed to keep their flesh in health, or to know what health is until they have ruined some vital organ, and so banished it forever.

I have not ruined any of my vital organs, and I appreciate what health is. I have grasped the art, the poetry of my fine feminine body.

This at the age of nineteen is a triumph for me.

Sometime in the midst of the brightness of an October I have walked for miles in the still high air under the blue of the sky. The brightness of the day and the blue of the sky and the incomparable high air have entered into my veins and flowed with my red blood. They have penetrated into every remote nerve-center and into the marrow of my bones.

At such a time this young body glows with life.

My red blood flows swiftly and joyously—in the midst of the brightness of October.

My sound, sensitive liver rests gently with its thin yellow bile in sweet content.

My calm, beautiful stomach silently sings, as I walk, a song of peace.

My lungs, saturated with mountain ozone and the perfume of the pines, expand in continuous ecstasy.

My heart beats like the music of Schumann, in easy, graceful rhythm with an undertone of power.

My strong and sensitive nerves are reeking and swimming in sensuality like drunken little Bacchantes, gay and garlanded in mad revelling.

The entire wonderful, graceful mechanism of my woman's-body has fallen at the time—like the wonderful, graceful mechanism of my woman's-mind—under the enchanting spell of a day in October.

"It is good," I think to myself, "oh, it is good to be alive! It is wondrously good to be a woman young in the fullness of nineteen springs. It is unutterably lovely to be a healthy young animal living on this charmed earth."

After I have walked for several hours I reach a region where the sulphur smoke has not penetrated, and I sit on the ground with drawn-up knees and rest as the shadows lengthen. The shadows lengthen early in October.

Presently I lie flat on my back and stretch my lithe slimness to its utmost like a mountain lioness taking her comfort. I am intensely thankful to the Devil for my two good legs and the full use of them under a short skirt, when, as now, they carry me out beyond the pale of civilization away from tiresome dull people. There is nothing in the world that can become so maddeningly wearisome as people, people, people!

And so, Devil, accept, for my two good legs, my sincerest gratitude. I lie on the ground for some minutes and meditate idly. There is a worldful of easy indolent, beautiful sensuality in the figure of a voting woman lying on the ground under a warm setting sun. A man may lie on the ground—but that is as far as it goes. A man would go to sleep, probably, like a dog or a pig. He would even snore, perhaps—under the setting sun. But then, a man has not a good young feminine body to feel with, to receive into itself the spirit of a warm sun at its setting, on a day in October,—and so let us forgive him for sleeping, and for snoring.

When I rise again to a sitting posture all the brightness has focused itself to the west. It casts a yellow glamour over the earth, a glamour not of joy, nor of pleasure, nor of happiness—but of peace.

The young poplar trees smile gently in the deathly still air.

The sage brush and the tall grass take on a radiant quietness. The high hills of Montana, near and distant, appear tender and benign. All is peace—peace. I think of that beautiful old song:

Sweet vale of Avoca! how calm could I rest
In thy bosom of shade——.

But I am too young yet to think of peace. It is not peace that I want. Peace is for forty and fifty. I am waiting for my Experience.

I am awaiting the coming of the Devil.

And now, just before twilight, after the sun has vanished over the edge, is the red, red line on the sky.

There will be days wild and stormy, filled with rain and wind and hail; and yet nearly always at the sun's setting there will be calm—and the red line of sky.

There is nothing in the world quite like this red sky at sunset. It is Glory, Triumph, Love, Fame!

Imagine a life bereft of things, and fingers pointed at it, and eyebrows raised; tossed and bandied hither and yon; crushed, beaten, bled, rent asunder, outraged, convulsed with pain; and then, into this life while still young, the red, red line of sky!

Why did I cry out against Fate, says the line; why did I rebel against my term of anguish! I now rather rejoice at it; now in my Happiness I remember it only with deep pleasure.

Think of that wonderful, admirable, matchless man of steel, Napoleon Bonaparte. He threw himself heavily on the world, and the world has never since been the same. He hated himself, and the world, and God, and Fate, and the Devil. His hatred was his term of anguish.

Then the sun threw on the sky for him a red, red line—the red line of Triumph, Glory, Fame!

And afterward there was the blackness of Night, the blackness that is not tender, not gentle.

But black as our Night may be, nothing can take from us the memory of the red, red sky. "Memory is possession," and so the red sky we have with us always.

Oh, Devil, Fate, World—some one, bring me my red sky! For a little brief time, and I will be satisfied. Bring it to me intensely red, intensely full, intensely alive! Short as you will, but red, red, red!

I am weary—weary, and, oh, I want my red sky! Short as it might be, its memory, its fragrance would stay with me always—always. Bring me, Devil, my red line of sky for one hour and take all, all—everything I possess. Let me keep my Happiness for one short hour, and take away all from me forever. I will be satisfied when Night has come and everything is gone.

Oh, I await you, Devil, in a wild frenzy of impatience!

And as I hurry back through the cool darkness of October, I feel this frenzy in every fiber of my fervid woman's-body.

19 JANUARY.

I COME from a long line of Scotch and Canadian MacLanes. There are a great many MacLanes, but there is usually only one real MacLane in each generation. There is but one who feels again the passionate spirit of the clans, those barbaric dwellers in the bleak, but well-beloved Highlands of Scotland.

I am the real MacLane of my generation. The real MacLane in these later centuries is always a woman. The men of the family never amount to anything worth naming—if one accepts the acme, the zenith, of pure selfishness, with a large letter "s." Life may be easy enough for the innumerable Canadian MacLanes who are not real. But it is certain to be more or less a Hill of Difficulty for the one who is. She finds herself somewhat alone. I have brothers and a sister and a mother in the same house with me—and I find myself somewhat alone. Between them and me there is no tenderness, no sympathy, no binding ties. Would it affect me in the least—do you suppose—if they should all die to-morrow? If I were not a real MacLane perhaps it would have been different, or perhaps I should not have missed these things.

How much, Devil, have I lost for the privilege of being a real MacLane?

But yes, I have also gained much.

20 JANUARY.

I HAVE said that I am alone.

I am not quite, quite alone.

I have one friend—of that Friendship that is real and is inlaid with the beautiful thing Truth. And because it has the beautiful thing Truth in it, this my one Friendship is somehow above and beyond me; there is something in it that I reach after in vain—for I have not that divinely beautiful thing Truth. Have I not said that I am a thief and a liar? But in this Friendship nevertheless there is a rare, ineffably sweet something that is mine. It is the one tender thing in this dull dreariness that wraps me round.

Are there many things in this cool-hearted world so utterly exquisite as the pure love of one woman for another woman?

My one friend is a woman some twelve or thirteen years older than I.

She is as different from me as is day from night. She believes in God—that God that is shown in the Bible of the Christians. And she carries with her an atmosphere of gentleness and truth. The while I am ready and waiting to dedicate my life to the Devil in exchange for Happiness—or some lesser thing. But I love Fannie Corbin with a peculiar and vivid intensity, and with all the sincerity and passion that is in me. Often I think of her, as I walk over the sand in my Nothingness, all day long. The Friendship of her and me is a fair, dear benediction upon me, but there is something in it—deep within it—that eludes me. In moments when I realize this, when I strain and reach vainly at a thing beyond me, when indeed I see in my mind a vision of the personality of Fannie Corbin, it is then that it comes on me with force that I am not good.

But I can love her with all the ardor of a young and passionate heart.

Yes, I can do that.

For a year I have loved my one friend. During the eighteen years of my life before she came into it I loved no one, for there was no one.

It is an extremely hard thing to go through eighteen years with no one to love, and no one to love you—the first eighteen years.

But now I have my one friend to love and to worship.

I have named my friend the "anemone lady," a name beautifully appropriate.

The anemone lady used to teach me literature in the Butte High School. She used to read poetry in the classroom in a clear, sweet voice that made one wish one might sit there forever and listen to it.

But now I have left the high school, and the dear anemone lady has gone from Butte. Before she went she told me she would be my friend.

Think of it—to live and have a friend!

My friend does not fully understand me; she thinks much too well of me. She has not a correct idea of my soul's depths and shallows. But if she did know them she would still be my friend. She knows the heavy weight of my unrest and unhappiness. She is tenderly sympathetic. She is the one in all the world who is dear to me.

Often I think, if only I could have my anemone lady and go and live with her in some little out-of-the-world place high up on the side of a mountain for the rest of my life—what more would I desire? My friendship would constitute my life. The unrest, the dreariness, the Nothingness of my existence now is so dull and gray by contrast that there would be Happiness for me in that life, Happiness softly radiant, if quiet—redolent of the fresh, thin fragrance of the dear blue anemone that grows in the winds and rains of spring.

But Miss Corbin would doubtless look somewhat askance

at the idea of spending the rest of her life with me on a mountain. She is very fond of me, but her feeling for me is not like mine for her, which indeed is natural. And her life is made up mostly of sacrifices—doing for her fellow-creatures, giving of herself. She never would leave this.

And so, then, the mountainside and the solitude and the friend with me are, like every good thing, but a vision.

"Thy friend is always thy friend; not to have, nor to hold, nor to love, nor to rejoice in: but to remember."

And so do I remember my one friend, the anemone lady—and think often about her with passionate love.

21 JANUARY.

HAPPINESS, don't you know, is of three kinds—and all are transitory. It never stays, but it comes and goes.

There is that happiness that comes from newly-washed feet, for instance, and a pair of clean stockings on them, particularly after one has been upon a tramp into the country. Always I have identified this kind of happiness with a Maltese cat, dipping a hungry, stealthy, sensual tongue into a bowl of fresh, thick cream.

There is that still happiness that has come to me at rare times when I have been with my one friend—and which does very well for people whose feelings are moderate. They need wish for nothing beyond it. They could not appreciate anything deeper.

And there is that kind of happiness which is of the red sunset sky. There is something terrible in the thought of this indescribable mad Happiness. What a thing it is for a human being to be *happy*—with the red, red Happiness of the sunset sky!

It's like a terrific storm in summer with rain and wind, beating quiet water into wild waves, bending great trees to the ground,—convulsing the green earth with delicious pain.

It's like something of Schubert's played on the violin that stirs you within to exquisite torture.

It's like the human voice divine singing a Scotch ballad in a manner to drag your soul from your body.

But there are no words to tell it. It is something infinitely above and beyond words. It is the kind of Happiness the Devil will bring to me when he comes,—to me, to *me!* Oh, why does he not come now when I am in the midst of my youth! Why is he so long in coming?

Often you hear a dozen stories of how the Devil was most ready and willing to take all from some one and give him his measure of Happiness. And sometimes the person was innately virtuous and so could not take the Happiness when it was offered. But Happiness is its own justification, and it should be eagerly grasped when it comes.

A world filled with fools will never learn this.

And so here I stand in the midst of Nothingness waiting and longing for the Devil, and he doesn't come. I feel a choking, strangling, frenzied feeling of waiting—oh, why doesn't my Happiness come! I have waited so long—so long.

There are persons who say to me that I ought not to think of the Devil, that I ought not to think of Happiness—Happiness for me would be sure to mean something wicked (as if Happiness could ever be wicked!); that I ought to think of being good. I ought to think of God. These are persons who help to fill the world with fools. At any rate their words are unable to affect me. I can not distinguish between right and wrong in this scheme of things. It is one of the lines of reasoning in which I have gotten to the edge, the end. I have gotten to the point to which all logic finally leads. I can only say, What is wrong? What is right? What is good? What is evil? The words are merely words, with word-meanings.

Truth is Love, and Love is the only Truth, and Love is the one thing out of all that is real.

The Devil is really the only one to whom we may turn, and he exacts payment in full for every favor.

But surely he will come one day with Happiness for me.

Yet, oh, how can I wait!

To be a woman, young and all alone, is hard—*hard!*—is to want things, is to carry a heavy, heavy weight.

Oh, damn! damn! damn! Damn every living thing, the world!—the universe be damned!

Oh, I am weary, weary! Can't you see that I am weary and pity me in my own damnation?

22 JANUARY.

IT IS night. I might well be in my bed taking a needed rest. But first I shall write.

Today I walked far away over the sand in the teeth of a bitter wind. The wind was determined that I should turn and come back, and equally I was determined I would go on. I went on.

There is a certain kind of wind in the autumn to walk in the midst of which causes one's spirits to rise ecstatically. To walk in the midst of a bitter wind in January may have almost any effect.

Today the bitter wind swept over me and around me and into the remote corners of my brain and swept away the delusions, and buffeted my philosophy with rough insolence.

The world is made up mostly of nothing. You may be convinced of this when a bitter wind has swept away your delusions.

What is the wind?

Nothing.

What is the sky?

Nothing.

What do we know?

Nothing.

What is fame?

Nothing.

What is my heart?

Nothing.

What is my soul?

Nothing.

What are we?

We are nothing.

We think we progress wonderfully in the arts and sciences as one century follows another. What does it amount to? It does not teach us the all-why. It does not let us cease to wonder what it is that we are doing, where it is that we are going. It does not teach us why the green comes again to the old, old hills in the spring; why the benign balm-o'-Gilead shines wet and sweet after the rain; why the red never fails to come to the breast of the robin, the black to the crow, the gray to the little wren; why the sand and barrenness lies stretched out around us; why the clouds float high above us; why the moon stands in the sky, night after night; why the mountains and valleys live on as the years pass.

The arts and sciences go on and on—still we wonder. We have not yet ceased to weep. And we suffer still in 1902, even as they suffered in 1802, and in 802.

Today we eat our good dinners with forks.

A thousand years ago they had no forks.

Yet, though we have forks, we are not happy. We scream and kick and struggle and weep just as they did a thousand years ago—when they had no forks.

We are "no wiser than when Omar fell asleep."

And in the midst of our great wondering, we wonder why some of us are given faith to trust without question, while the rest of us are left to eat out our life's vitals with asking.

I have walked once in summer by the side of a little marsh filled with mint and white hawthorn. The mint and white hawthorn have with them a vivid, rare, delicious perfume. It makes you want to grovel on the ground—it makes you think you might crawl in the dust all your days, and well for you. The perfume lingers with you afterward when years have passed. You may scream and kick and struggle and weep right lustily every day of your life, but in your moments of calmness sometimes there will come back to you the fragrance of a swamp filled with mint and white hawthorn.

It is meltingly beautiful.

What does it mean?

What would it tell?

Why does the marsh, and the mint and white hawthorn, freeze over in the fall? And why do they come again, voluptuous, enticing, in the damp spring days—and rack the souls of wretches who look and wonder?

You are superb, Devil! You have done a magnificent piece of work. I kneel at your feet and worship you. You have wrought a perfection, a pinnacle of fine, invisible damnation.

The world is like a little marsh filled with mint and white hawthorn. It is filled with things likewise damnably beautiful. There are the green, green grass-blades and the gray dawns;

there are swiftly-flowing rivers and the honking of wild geese, flying low; there are human voices and human eyes; there are stories of women and men who have learned to give up and to wait; there is poetry; there is Charity; there is Truth.

The Devil has made all of these things, and also he has made human beings who can feel.

Who was it that said, long ago, "Life is always a tragedy to those who feel"?

In truth, the Devil has constructed a place of infinite torture—the fair green earth, the world. But he has made that other infinite thing—Happiness. I forgive him for making me wonder, since possibly he may bring me Happiness. I cast myself at his feet. I adore him.

The first third of our lives is spent in the expectation of Happiness. Then it comes, perhaps, and stays ten years, or a month, or three days, and the rest of our lives is spent in peace and rest—with the memory of the Happiness.

Happiness—though it is infinite—is a transient emotion.

It is too brilliant, too magnificent, too overwhelming to be a lasting thing. And it is merely an emotion. But, ah—*such* an emotion! Through it the Devil rules his domains. What would one not do to have it!

I can think of no so-called vile deed that I would scruple about if I could be happy. Everything is justified if it gives me Happiness. The Devil has done me some great favors; he has made me without a conscience, and without Virtue.

For which I thank thee, Devil.

At least I shall be able to take my Happiness when it comes—even though the piles of nice distinctions between it and me be mountains high.

But meanwhile, the world, I say, and the people are nothing, nothing, nothing. The splendid castles, the strong bridges, that we are building are of small moment. We can only go down the wide roadway wondering and weeping, and without where to lay our heads.

I HAVE eaten my dinner.

I have had, among other things, fine, rare-broiled porterhouse steak from Omaha, and some fresh, green young onions from California. And just now I am a philosopher, pure and simple—except that there's nothing very pure about my philosophy, nor yet very simple.

Let the Devil come and go; let the wild waters rush over me; let nations rise and fall; let my favorite theories form themselves in line suddenly and run into the ground; let the little earth be bandied about from one belief to another; but, I say in the midst of my young peripatetic philosophy, I need not be in complete despair—the world still contains things for me, while I have my fine rare porterhouse steak from Omaha—and my fresh green young onions from California.

Fame may pass over my head; money may escape me; my one friend may fail me; every hope may fold its tent and steal away; Happiness may remain a sealed book; every remnant of human ties may vanish; I may find myself an outcast; good things held out to me may suddenly be withdrawn; the stars may go out, one by one; the sun may go dark; yet still I may hold upright my head, if I have but my steak—and my onions.

I may find myself crowded out from many charmed circles; I may find the ethical world too small to contain me; the social world may also exclude me; the professional world may know me not; likewise the worlds of the arts and the sciences; I may find myself superfluous in literary haunts; I may see myself going gladly back to the vile dust from whence I sprung—to live in a green forest like the melancholy Jacques; but fare they well, I will say with what cheerfulness I can summon, while I have my steak—and my onions.

Possibly I may grow old and decrepit; my hair may turn gray; my bones may become rheumatic; I may grow weak in the knees; my ankle-joints which have withstood many a peripatetic journey may develop dropsical tendencies; my heart may miss a beat now and then; my lungs may begin to fight shy of wintry blasts; my eyes may fail me; my figure that is now in its slim gracefulness may swathe itself in layers of flesh, or worse, it may wither and decay and stoop at the shoulders; my red blood may flow sluggishly; but if I still have left teeth to eat with, why need I lament while I have my steak—and my onions?

I am obscure; I am morbid; I am unhappy; my life is made up of Nothingness; I want everything and I have nothing; I have been made to feel the "lure of green things growing," and I have been made to feel also that something of them is withheld from me; I have felt the deadly tiredness that is among the birthrights of a human being; but with it all the Devil has given me a philosophy of my own—the Devil has enabled me to count, if need be, the world well lost for a fine rare porterhouse steak—and some green young onions.

For which I thank thee, Devil, profoundly.

Who says the Devil is not your friend? Who says the Devil does not believe in the all-merciful Law of Compensation?

And so it is—do you see?—that all things look different after a satisfying dinner, that the color of the world changes, that life in fact resolves itself into two things: a fine rare-broiled porterhouse steak from Omaha, and some fresh green young onions from California.

24 JANUARY.

I AM charmingly original. I am delightfully refreshing. I am startlingly Bohemian. I am quaintly interesting—the while in my sleeve I may be smiling and smiling—and a villain. I can talk to a roomful of dull people and compel their interest, admiration, and astonishment. I do this sometimes for my own amusement. As I have said, I am a rather plain-featured, insignificant-looking genius, but I have a graceful personality. I have a pretty figure. And when I choose to talk in my charmingly original fashion, embellishing my conversation with many quaint lies, I have a certain very noticeable way with me, an "air."

It is well, if one has nothing else, to acquire an air. And an air taken in conjunction with my charming originality, my delightfully refreshing candor, is something powerful and striking in its way.

I do not, however, exert myself often in this way; partly

because I can sometimes foresee, from the character of the assembled company, that my performance will not have the desired effect—for I am a genius, and genius at close range at times carries itself unconsciously to the point where it becomes so interesting that it is atrocious, and can not be carried farther without having somewhat mildly disastrous results; and then, again, the facial antics of some ten or a dozen persons possessed more or less of the qualities of the genus fool—even they become tiresome after a while.

Always I talk about myself on an occasion of this kind. Indeed, my conversation is on all occasions devoted directly or indirectly to myself.

When I talk on the subject of ethics, I talk of it as it is related to Mary MacLane.

When I give out broad-minded opinions about Ninon de l'Enclos, I demonstrate her relative position to Mary MacLane!

When I discourse liberally on the subject of the married relation, I talk of it only as it will affect Mary MacLane.

An interesting creature, Mary MacLane.

As a matter of fact, it is so with every one, only every one is far from realizing and acknowledging it. And I have not lacked listeners, though these people do not appreciate me. They do not realize that I am a genius.

I am of womankind and of nineteen years. I am able to stand off and gaze critically and dispassionately at myself and my relation to my environment, to the world, to everything the world contains. I am able to judge whether I am good and whether I am bad. I am able, indeed, to tell what I am and where I stand. I can see far, far inward. I am a genius.

Charlotte Brontë did this in some degree, and she was a genius; and also Marie Bashkirtseff, and Olive Schreiner, and George Eliot. They are all geniuses.

And so, then, I am a genius—a genius in my own right.

I am fundamentally, organically egotistic. My vanity and self-conceit have attained truly remarkable development as I've walked and walked in the loneliness of the sand and barrenness. Not the least remarkable part of it is that I know my egotism and vanity thoroughly—thoroughly, and plume myself thereon.

These are the ear-marks of a genius—and of a fool. There is

a finely-drawn line between a genius and a fool. Often this line is overstepped and your fool becomes a genius, or your genius becomes a fool.

It is but a tiny step.

There's but a tiny step between the great and the little, the tender and the contemptuous, the sublime and the ridiculous, the aggressive and the humble, the paradise and the perdition.

And so is it between the genius and the fool.

I am a genius.

I am not prepared to say how many times I may overstep the finely-drawn line, or how many times I have already overstepped it. 'Tis a matter of small moment.

I have entered into certain things marvelously deep. I know things, I know that I know them, and I know that I know that I know them, which is a fine psychological point.

It is magnificent of me to have gotten so far, at the age of nineteen, with no training other than that of the sand and barrenness. Magnificent—do you hear?

Very often I take this fact in my hand and squeeze it hard like an orange, to get the sweet, sweet juice from it. I squeeze a great deal of juice from it every day, and every day the juice is renewed, like the vitals of Prometheus. And so I squeeze and squeeze, and drink the juice, and try to be satisfied.

Yes, you may gaze long and curiously at the portrait in the front of this book. It is of one who is a genius of egotism and analysis, a genius who is awaiting the Devil's coming,—a genius, with a wondrous liver within.

I shall tell you more about this liver, I think, before I have done.

25 JANUARY.

I CAN remember a time long, oh, very long ago. That is the time when I was a child. It is ten or a dozen years ago.

Or is it a thousand years ago?

It is when you have but just parted from your friend that he seems farthest from you. When I have lived several more years the time when I was a child will not seem so far behind me.

Just now it is frightfully far away. It is so far away that I can see it plainly outlined on the horizon.

It is there always for me to look at. And when I look I can feel the tears deep within me—a salt ocean of tears that roll and surge and swell bitterly in a dull, mad anguish, and never come to the surface.

I do not know which is the more weirdly and damnably pathetic: I when I was a child, or I when I am grown to a woman, young and all alone. I weigh the question coldly and logically, but my logic trembles with rage and grief and unhappiness.

When I was a child I lived in Canada and in Minnesota. I was a little wild savage. In Minnesota there were swamps where I used to wet my feet in the spring, and there were fields of tall grass where I would lie flat on my stomach in company with lizards and little garter snakes. And there were poplar leaves that turned their pale green backs upward on a hot afternoon, and soon there would be terrific thunder and lightning and rain. And there were robins that sang at dawn. These things stay with one always. And there were children with whom I used to play and fight.

I was tanned and sunburned, and I had an unkempt appearance. My face was very dirty. The original pattern of my frock was invariably lost in layers and vistas of the native soil. My hair was braided or else it flew about, a tangled maze, according as I could be caught by some one and rubbed and straightened before I ran away for the day. My hands were little and strong and brown, and wrought much mischief. I came and went at my own pleasure. I ate what I pleased; I went to bed all in my own good time; I tramped wherever my stubborn little feet chose. I was impudent; I was contrary; I had an extremely bad temper; I was hard-hearted; I was full of infantile malice. Truly I was a vicious little beast.

I was a little piece of untrained Nature.

And I am unable to judge which is the more savagely forlorn: the starved-hearted child, or the woman, young and all alone.

The little wild stubborn child felt things and wanted things. She did not know that she felt things and wanted things.

Now I feel and I want things and I know it with burning vividness.

The little vicious Mary MacLane suffered, but she did not know that she suffered. Yet that did not make the suffering less.

And she reached out with a little sunburned hand to touch and take something.

But the sunburned little hand remained empty. There was nothing for it. No one had anything to put into it.

The little wild creature wanted to be loved; she wanted something to put in her hungry little heart.

But no one had anything to put into a hungry little heart.

No one said "dear."

The little vicious child was the only MacLane, and she felt somewhat alone. But there, after all, were the lizards and the little garter snakes.

The wretched, hardened little piece of untrained Nature has grown and developed into a woman, young and alone. For the child there was a Nothingness, and for the woman there is a great Nothingness.

Perhaps the Devil will bring me something in my lonely womanhood to put in my wooden heart.

But the time when I was a child will never come again. It is gone—gone. I may live through some long, long years, but nothing like it will ever come. For there is nothing like it.

It is a life by itself. It has naught to do with philosophy, or with genius, or with heights, and depths, or with the red sunset sky, or with the Devil.

These come later.

The time of the child is a thing apart. It is the Planting and Seed-time. It is the Beginning of things. It decides whether there shall be brightness or bitterness in the long after-years.

I have left that time far enough behind me. It will never come back. And it had a Nothingness—do you hear, a *Nothingness!* Oh, the pity of it! the pity of it!

Do you know why it is that I look back to the horizon at the figure of an unkempt, rough child, and why I feel a surging torrent of tears and anguish and despair?

I feel more than that indeed, but I have no words to tell it.

I shall have to miss forever some beautiful, wonderful

things because of that wretched, lonely childhood.

There will always be a lacking, a wanting—some dead branches that never grew leaves.

It is not deaths and murders and plots and wars that make life tragedy.

It is Nothing that makes life tragedy.

It is day after day, and year after year, and Nothing.

It is a sunburned little hand reached out and Nothing put into it.

26 JANUARY.

I SIT at my window and look out upon the housetops and chimneys of Butte. As I look I have a weary, disgusted feeling.

People are abominable creatures.

Under each of the roofs live a man and woman joined together by that very slender thread, the marriage ceremony—and their children, the result of the marriage ceremony.

How many of them love each other? Not two in a hundred, I warrant. The marriage ceremony is their one miserable, petty, paltry excuse for living together.

This marriage rite, it appears, is often used as a cloak to cover a world of rather shameful things.

How virtuous these people are, to be sure, under their different roof-trees. So virtuous are they indeed that they are able to draw themselves up in the pride of their own purity, when they happen upon some corner where the marriage ceremony is lacking. So virtuous are they that the men can afford to find amusement and diversion in the woes of the corner that is without the marriage rite; and the women may draw away their skirts in shocked horror and wonder that such things can be, in view of their own spotless virtue.

And so they live on under the roofs, and they eat and work and sleep and die; and the children grow up and seek other roofs, and call upon the marriage ceremony even as their parents before them—and then they likewise eat and work and sleep and die; and so on world without end.

This also is life—the life of the good, virtuous Christians.

I think, therefore, that I should prefer some life that is not virtuous.

I shall never make use of the marriage ceremony. I hereby register a vow, Devil, to that effect.

When a man and a woman love one another that is enough. That is marriage. A religious rite is superfluous. And if the man and woman live together without the love, no ceremony in the world can make it marriage. The woman who does this need not feel the tiniest bit better than her lowest sister in the streets. Is she not indeed a step lower since she pretends to be what she is not—plays the virtuous woman? While the other unfortunate pretends nothing. She wears her name on her sleeve.

If I were obliged to be one of these I would rather be she who wears her name on her sleeve. I certainly would. The lesser of two evils, always.

I can think of nothing in the world like the utter littleness, the paltriness, the contemptibleness, the degradation, of the woman who is tied down under a roof with a man who is really nothing to her; who wears the man's name, who bears the man's children—who plays the virtuous woman. There are too many such in the world now.

May I never, I say, become that abnormal, merciless animal, that deformed monstrosity—a virtuous woman.

Anything, Devil, but that.

And so, as I look out over the roofs and chimneys, I have a weary, disgusted feeling.

27 JANUARY.

THIS is not a diary. It is a Portrayal. It is my inner life shown in its nakedness. I am trying my utmost to show everything—to reveal every petty vanity and weakness, every phase of feeling, every desire. It is a remarkably hard thing to do, I find, to probe my soul to its depths, to expose its shades and half-lights.

Not that I am troubled with modesty, or shame. Why should one be ashamed of anything?

But there are elements in one's mental equipment so vague, so opaque, so undefined—how is one to grasp them? I have analyzed and analyzed, and I have gotten down to some extremely fine points—yet still there are things upon my own horizon that go beyond me.

There are feelings that rise and rush over me overwhelmingly. I am helpless, crushed, and defeated, before them. It is as if they were written on the walls of my soul-chamber in an unknown language.

My soul goes blindly seeking, seeking, asking. Nothing answers. I cry out after some unknown Thing with all the strength of my being; every nerve and fiber in my young woman's-body and my young woman's-soul reaches and strains in anguished unrest. At times as I hurry over my sand and barrenness all my life's manifold passions culminate in utter rage and woe. Waves of intense, hopeless longing rush over me and envelop me round and round. My heart, my soul, my mind go wandering—wandering; ploughing their way through darkness with never a ray of light; groping with helpless hands; asking, longing, wanting things: pursued by a Demon of Unrest.

I shall go mad—I shall go mad, I say over and over to myself.

But no. No one goes mad. The Devil does not propose to release any one from a so beautifully-wrought, artistic damnation. He looks to it that one's senses are kept fully intact, and he fastens to them with steel chains the Demon of Unrest.

It hurts—oh, it tortures me in the days and days! But when the Devil brings me my Happiness I will forgive him all this.

When my Happiness is given me, the Unrest will still be with me, I doubt not, but the Happiness will change the tenor of it, will make it an instrument of joy, will clasp hands with it and mingle itself with it,—the while I, with my wooden heart, my woman's-body, my mind, my soul, shall be in transports. I shall be filled with pleasure so deep and pain so intense that my being's minutest nerve will reel and stagger in intoxication, will go drunk with the fullness of Life.

When my Happiness is given me I shall live centuries in the hours. And we shall all grow old rapidly,—I and my wooden heart, and my woman's-body, and my mind, and my soul. Sorrow may age one in some degree. But Happiness—the real Happiness—rolls countless years off from one's fingertips in a single moment, and each year leaves its impress.

It is true that life is a tragedy to those who feel. When my Happiness is given me life will be an ineffable, a nameless thing.

It will seethe and roar; it will plunge and whirl; it will leap and shriek in convulsion; it will quiver in delicate fantasy; it will writhe and twist; it will glitter and flash and shine; it will sing gently; it will shout in exquisite excitement; it will vibrate to the roots like a great oak in a storm; it will dance; it will glide; it will gallop; it will rush; it will swell and surge; it will fly; it will soar high—high; it will go down into depths unexplored; it will rage and rave; it will yell in utter joy; it will melt; it will blaze; it will ride triumphant; it will grovel in the dust of entire pleasure; it will sound out like a terrific blare of trumpets; it will chime faintly, faintly like the remote tinkling notes of a harp; it will sob and grieve and weep; it will revel and carouse; it will shrink; it will go in pride; it will lie prone like the dead; it will float buoyantly on air; it will moan, shiver, burst—oh, it will reek with Love and Light!

The words of the English language are futile. There are no words in it, or in any other, to express an idea of that thing which would be my life in its Happiness.

The words I have written describe it, it is true,—but confusedly and inadequately.

But words are for everyday use.

When it comes my turn to meet face to face the unspeakable vision of the Happy Life I shall be rendered dumb.

But the rains of my feeling will come in torrents!

28 JANUARY.

I AM an artist of the most artistic, the highest type. I have uncovered for myself the art that lies in obscure shadows. I have discovered the art of the day of small things.

And that surely is art with a capital "A."

I have acquired the art of Good Eating. Usually it is in the gray and elderly forties and fifties that people cultivate this art—

if they ever do; it is indeed a rare art.

But I know it in all its rare exquisiteness at the young slim age of nineteen—which is one more mark of my genius, do you see?

The art of Good Eating has two essential points: one must eat only when one is hungry, and one must take small bites.

There are persons who eat for the sake of eating. They are gourmands, and partake of the natures of the pig and the buzzard. There are persons who take bites that are not small. These also are gourmands and partake of the natures of the pig and the buzzard. There are persons who can enjoy nothing in the way of eating except a luxurious, well-appointed meal. These, it is safe to say, have not acquired the art of anything.

But I—I have acquired the art of eating an olive.

Now listen, and I will tell you the art of eating an olive:

I take the olive in my fingers, and I contemplate its green oval richness. It makes me think at once of the land where the green citron grows—where the cypress and myrtle are emblems; of the land of the Sun where human beings are delightfully, enchantingly wicked,—where the men are eager and passionate, and the women gracefully developed in mind and in body—and their two breasts show round and full and delicately veined beneath thin drapery.

The mere sight of the olive conjures up this charming picture in my mind.

I set my teeth and my tongue upon the olive, and bite it. It is bitter, salt, delicious. The saliva rushes to meet it, and my tongue is a happy tongue. As the morsel of olive rests in my mouth and is crunched and squeezed lusciously among my teeth, a quick, temporary change takes place in my character. I think of some adorable lines of the Persian poet: "Give thyself up to joy, for thy Grief will be infinite. The stars shall again meet together at the same point in the firmament, but of thy body shall bricks be made for a palace wall."

"Oh, dear, sweet, bitter olive!" I say to myself.

The bit of olive slips down my red gullet, and so into my stomach. There it meets with a joyous welcome. Gastric juices leap out from the walls and swathe it in loving embrace. My stomach is fond of something bitter and salt. It lavishes flattery and endearment galore upon the olive. It laughs in silent delight. It feels that the day it has long waited for has come. The philosophy of my stomach is wholly epicurean. Let it receive but a tiny bit of olive and it will reck not of the morrow, nor of the past. It lives, voluptuously, in the present. It is content. It is in paradise.

I bite the olive again. Again the bitter salt crisp ravishes my tongue. "If this be vanity,—vanity let it be." The golden moments flit by and I heed them not. For am I not comfortably seated and eating an olive? Go hang yourself, you who have never been comfortably seated and eating an olive! My character evolves farther in its change. I am now bent on reckless sensuality, let happen what will. The fair earth seems to resolve itself into a thing oval and crisp and good and green and deliciously salt. I experience a feeling of fervent gladness that I am a female thing living, and that I have a tongue and some teeth, and salivary glands.

Also this bit slips down my red gullet, and again the festive Stomach lifts up a silent voice in psalms and rejoicing. It is now an absolute monarchy with the green olive at its head. The kisses of the gastric juice become hot and sensual and convulsive and ecstatic. "Avaunt, pale, shadowy ghosts of dyspepsia!" says my Stomach. "I know you not. I am of a brilliant, shining world. I dwell in Elysian fields."

Once more I bite the olive. Once more is my tongue electrified. And the third stage in my temporary transformation takes place. I am now a gross but supremely contented sensualist. An exquisite symphony of sensualism and pleasure seems to play somewhere within me. My heart purrs. My brain folds its arms and lounges. I put my feet up on the seat of another chair. The entire world is now surely one delicious green olive. My mind is capable of conceiving but one idea—that of a green olive. Therefore the green olive is a perfect thing—absolutely a perfect thing.

Disgust and disapproval are excited only by imperfections. When a thing is perfect, no matter how hard one may look at it, one can see only itself—itself, and nothing beyond.

And so I have made my olive and my art perfect.

Well, then, this third bit of olive slides down the willing gullet into my stomach. "And then my heart with pleasure fills."

The play of the gastric secretions is now marvelous. It is the meeting of the waters! It were well, ah, how well, if the hearts of the world could mingle in peace, as the gastric juices mingle at the coming of a green olive into my stomach! "Paradise! Paradise!" says my Stomach.

Every drop of blood in my passionate veins is resting. Through my stomach—my *stomach*, do you hear—my soul seems to feel the infinite. The minutes are flying. Shortly it will be over. But just now I am safe. I am entirely satisfied. I want nothing, nothing.

My inner quiet is infinite. I am conscious that it is but momentary, and it matters not. On the contrary, the knowledge of this fact renders the present quiet—the repose, more limitless, more intense.

Where now, Devil, is your damnation? If this be damnation, damnation let it be! If this be the human fall, then how good it is to be fallen! At this moment I would fain my fall were like yours, Lucifer, "never to hope again."

And so, bite by bite, the olive enters into my body and soul. Each bite brings with it a recurring wave of sensation and charm.

No. We will not dispute with the brilliant mind that declared life a tragedy to those who feel. We will let that stand. However, there are parts of the tragedy that are not tragic. There are parts that admit of a turning aside.

As the years pass, one after another, I shall continue to eat. And as I eat I shall have my quiet, my brief period of aberration.

This is the art of Eating.

I have acquired it by means of self-examination, analyzing—analyzing—analyzing. Truly my genius is analytical. And it enables me to endure—if also to feel bitterly—the heavy, heavy weight of life.

What a worm of misery I should be were it not for these bursts of philosophy, these turnings aside!

If it please the Devil, one day I may have Happiness. That will be all-sufficient. I shall then analyze no more. I shall be a different being.

But meanwhile I shall eat.

When the last of the olive vanishes into the stomach, when

it is there reduced to animated chyme, when I play with the olive-seed in my fingers, when I lean back in my chair and straighten out my spinal column,—oh, then do you not envy me, you fine, brave world, who are not a philosopher, who have not discovered the art of the small things, who have not conscious chyme in your stomach, who have not acquired the art of Good Eating!

29 JANUARY.

AS I read over now and then what I have written of my Portrayal I have alternate periods of hope and despair. At times I think I am succeeding admirably—and again, what I have written compared to what I have felt seems vapid and tame. Who has not felt the futility of words when one would express feelings?

I take this hope and despair as an other mark of genius. Genius, apart from natural sensitiveness, is prone equally to unreasoning joy and to bitterest morbidness.

I am more than fond of writing, though I have hours when I can not write any more than I could paint a picture, or play Wagner as it should be played.

I think my style of writing has a wonderful intensity in it, and it is admirably suited to the creature it portrays. What sort of Portrayal of myself would I produce if I wrote with the long, elaborate periods of Henry James, or with the pleasant, ladylike phrasing of Howells? It would be rather like a little tin phonograph trolling out flowery poetry at breakneck speed, or like a deep-toned church organ pouring forth "Goo-Goo Eyes" with ponderous feeling.

When I read a book I study it carefully to find whether the author *knows things*, and whether I could, with the same subject, write a better one myself.

The latter question I usually decide in the affirmative.

The highest thing one can do in literature is to succeed in saying that thing which one meant to say. There is nothing better than that—to make the world see your thoughts as you see them. Eugene Field and Edgar Allan Poe and Robert Louis

Stevenson and Charles Dickens, among others, have succeeded in doing this. They impress the world with a sense of their courage and realness.

There are people who have written books which did not impress the world in this way, but which nevertheless came out of the feeling and fullness of zealous hearts. Always I think of that pathetic, artless little old-fashioned thing, *Jane Eyre*, as a picture shown to a world seeing with distorted vision. Charlotte Brontë meant one thing when she wrote the book, and the world after a time suddenly understood a quite different thing, and heaped praise and applause upon her therefor. When I read the book I was not quite able to see just what the message was that the Brontë intended to send out. But I saw that there was a message—of bravery, perhaps, or of that good which may come out of Nazareth. But the world that praised and applauded and gave her money seems totally to have missed it.

It takes centuries of tears and piety and mourning to move this world a tiny bit.

But still it will give you praise and applause and money if you will prostitute your sensibilities and emotions for the gratification of it.

I have no message to hide in a book and send out. I am writing a Portrayal.

But a Portrayal is also a thing that may be misunderstood.

30 January.

AN IDLE brain is the Devil's workshop, they say. It is an absurdly incongruous statement. If the Devil is at work in a brain it certainly is not idle. And when one considers how brilliant a personage the Devil is, and what very fine work he turns out, it becomes an open question whether he would have the slightest use for most of the idle brains that cumber the earth. But, after all, the Devil is so clever that he could produce unexcelled workmanship with even the poorest tools.

My brain is one kind of devil's workshop, and it is as incessantly hard-worked and always-busy a one as you could imagine.

It is a devil's workshop, indeed, only I do the work myself. But there is a mental telegraphy between the Devil and me, which accounts for the fact that many of my ideas are so wonderfully groomed and perfumed and colored. I take no credit to myself for this, though, as I say, I do the work myself.

I try always to give the Devil his due—and particularly in this Portrayal.

There are very few who give the Devil his due in this world of hypocrites.

I never think of the Devil as that atrocious creature in red tights, with cloven hoofs and a tail and a two-tined fork. I think of him rather as an extremely fascinating, strong, steel-willed person in conventional clothes—a man with whom to fall completely, madly in love. I rather think, I believe, that he is incarnate at times. Why not?

Periodically I fall completely, madly in love with the Devil. He is so fascinating, so strong—so strong, exactly the sort of man whom my wooden heart awaits. I would like to throw myself at his head. I would make him a dear little wife. He would love me—he would love me. I would be in raptures. And I would love him, oh, madly, madly!

"What would you have me do, little MacLane?" the Devil would say.

"I would have you conquer me, crush me, know me," I would answer.

"What shall I say to you?" the Devil would ask.

"Say to me, 'I love you, I love you, I love you,' in your strong, steel, fascinating voice. Say it to me often, always—a million times."

"What would you have me do, little MacLane?" he would say again.

I would answer: "Hurt me, burn me, consume me with hot love, shake me violently, embrace me hard, *hard* in your strong, steel arms, kiss me with wonderful burning kisses—press your lips to mine with passion, and your soul and mine would meet then in an anguish of joy for me!"

"How shall I treat you, little MacLane?"

"Treat me cruelly, brutally."

"How long shall I stay with you?"

"Through the life everlasting—it will be as one day; or for one day—it will be as the life everlasting."

"And what kind of children will you bear me, little MacLane?" he would say.

"I will bear wonderful, beautiful children—with great pain."

"But you hate pain," the Devil will say, "and when you are in your pain you will hate me."

"But no," I will answer, "pain that comes of you whom I love will be ineffable exaltation."

"And how will you treat me, little MacLane?"

"I will cast myself at your feet; or I will minister to you with divine tenderness; or I will charm you with fantastic deviltry; when you weep, I will melt into tears; when you rejoice, I will go wild with delight; when you go deaf I will stop my ears; when you go blind I will put out my eyes; when you go lame I will cut off my legs. Oh, I will be divinely dear, unutterably sweet!"

"Indeed you are rarely sweet," the Devil will say. And I will be in transports.

Oh, Devil, Devil, Devil!

Oh, misery, *misery* of Nothingness!

The days are long—long and very weary as I await the Devil's coming.

31 January.

TODAY as I walked out I was impressed deeply with the wonderful beautifulness of Nature even in her barrenness. The far-distant mountains had that high, pure, transparent look, and the nearer ones were transformed completely with a wistful beseeching attitude that reminded me of my life. It was late in the afternoon. As the sun lowered, the pure lavender of the far-away hills was tinted with faint-rose, and the gray of the nearer ones with sun-color. And the sand—my sand and barrenness—almost flushed consciously in its wide, mysterious magnitude. In the sky there was a white cloud. The sky was blue—blue almost as when I was a child. The air was very gentle. The earth seemed softened. There was an indefinite, caressing something over all that went into my soul and stirred it, and hurt it. There was that in the air which is there when something is going to happen. Only nothing ever happens. It is rare, I thought, that my sand and barrenness looks like this. I crouched on the ground, and the wondrous calm and beauty of the natural things awed and moved me with strange, still emotions.

I felt, and gazed about me, and felt again. And everything was very still.

Presently my eyes filled quietly with tears.

I bent my head into the breast of a great gray rock. Oh, my soul, my soul, I said over and over, not with passion. It is so divine—the earth is so beautiful, so untainted—and I, what am I? It was so beautiful that now as I write, and it comes over me again, I can not restrain the tears.

Tears are not common.

I felt my wooden heart, my soul, quivering and sobbing with their unknown wanting. This is my soul's awakening. Ah, the pain of my soul's awakening! Is there nothing, nothing to help this pain? I am so lonely, so lonely—Fannie Corbin, my one friend, my dearly-loved anemone lady, I want you so much—why aren't you here! I want to feel your hand with mine as I felt it sometimes before you went away. You are the only one among a worldful of people to care a little—and I love you with all the strength and worship I can give to the things that are beautiful and true. You are the only one, the only one—and my soul is full of pain, and I am sitting alone on the ground, and my head lies on a rock's breast.—

Strange, sweet passions stirred and waked somewhere deep within me as I sat shivering on the ground. And I felt them singing far away, as if their faint voices came out of that limitless deep, deep blue above me; and it was like a choir of spirit-voices, and they sang of love and of light and of dear tender dreams, and of my soul's awakening. Why is this—and what is it that is hurting so? Is it because I am young, or is it because I am alone, or because I am a woman?

Oh, it is a hard and bitter thing to be a woman! And why—why? Is woman so foul a creature that she must needs be purged by this infinite pain?

The choir of faint, sweet voices comes to me incessantly out of the blue. My wooden heart and my soul are listening to them intently. The voices are trying hard to tell me, to help me, but I can not understand. I know only that it is about pure, exalted things, and about the all-abiding love that is somewhere; and it is about the earth-love, and about Truth,—but I can not understand. And the voices sing of me the child—a song of the unloved, starved little being; and a song of the unloved, half-grown creature; and a song of me, a woman and all alone—awaiting the Devil's coming.

Oh, my soul—my soul!

A female snake is born out of its mother's white egg, and lives awhile in content among weeds and grass, and dies.

A female dog lives some years, and has bones thrown at her, and sometimes she receives a kick or a blow, and a dog-house to sleep in, and dies.

A female bird has a nest, and worms to eat, and goes south in the winter, and presently she dies.

A female toad has a swamp or a garden, some bugs and flies, contentment—and then she dies.

And each of these has a male thing with her for a time, and soon there are little snakes or little dogs for her to love as much as it is given her to love—she can do no more.

And they are fortunate with their little snakes and little dogs.

A female human being is born out of her mother's fair body, branded with a strange, plague-tainted name, and let go; and lives awhile, and dies. But before she dies she awakes. There is a pain that goes with it.

And the male thing that is with her for a time is unlike a snake or a dog. It is more like a man, and there is another pain for this.

And when a little human being comes with a soul of its own there must be another awakening, for she has then reached the best and highest state that any human being can reach, though she is a female human being, and plague-tainted. And here also there is heavy soul-pain.

The name—the plague-tainted name branded upon her—

means woman.

I lifted my head from the breast of the gray rock. The tears had been falling, falling. Tears are so strange! Tears from the dried-up fountain of nineteen years are like drops of water wrung out of stone. Suddenly I got up from the ground and ran quickly over the sand for several minutes. I did not dare look again at the hilltops and the deep blue, nor listen again to the voices.

Oh, with it all, I am a coward! I shrink and cringe before the pain of the dazzling lights. Yet I am waiting—longing for the most dazzling light of all: the coming of the Devil.

1 FEBRUARY.

OH, THE wretched bitter loneliness of me!

In all the deep darkness, and the silence, there is never a faint human light, never a voice!

How can I bear it—how can I bear it!

2 FEBRUARY.

I HAVE been looking over the confessions of the Bashkirtseff. They are indeed rather like my Portrayal, but they are not so interesting, nor so intense. I have a stronger individuality than Marie Bashkirtseff, though her mind was probably in a higher state of development than mine, even when she was younger than I.

Most of her emotions are vacillating and inconsistent. She worships a God one day and blasphemes him the next. She never loves her God. And why, then, does she have a God? Why does she not abandon him altogether? He seems to be of no use to her—except as a convenient thing on which to fasten the blame for her misfortunes. And, after all, that is something very useful indeed.—And she loves the people about her one day, and the next day she hates them.

But in her great passion—her ambition, Marie Bashkirtseff was beautifully consistent. And what terrific storms of woe and despair must have enveloped her when she knew that within a certain period she would be dead—removed from the world, and her work left undone! The time kept creeping nearer—she must have tasted the bitterness of death indeed. She was sure of success, sure that her high-strained ambition would be gratified to its last vestige—and then, to die! It was certainly hard lines for the little Bashkirtseff.

My own despair is of an opposite nature.

There is one thing in the world that is more bitter than death—and that is life.

Suppose that I learned I was to die on the twenty-seventh of June, 1903, for instance. It would give me a soft warm wave of pleasure, I think. I might be in the depths of woe at the time; my despair might be the despair of despair; my misery utterly unceasing,—and I could say, Never mind, on the twenty-seventh of June, 1903, all will be over—dull misery, rage, Nothingness, obscurity, the unknown longing, every desire of my soul, all the pain—ended inevitably, completely on the twenty-seventh of June, 1903. I might come upon a new pain, but this, my long old torture, would cease.

You may say that I might end my life on that day, that I might do so now. I certainly shall if the pain becomes greater than I can bear—for what else is there to do? But I shall be far from satisfied in doing so. What if I were to end everything now—when perhaps the Devil may be coming to me in two years' time with Happiness?

Upon dying it might be that I should go to some wondrous fair country where there would be trees and running water, and a resting-place. Well—oh, well! But I want the earthly Happiness. I am not high-minded and spiritual. I am earthly, human—sensitive, sensuous, sensual, and, ah, dear, my soul wants its earthly Happiness!

I can not bring myself to the point of suicide while there is a possibility of Happiness remaining. But if I knew that irrevocable, inevitable death awaited me on June twenty-seventh, 1903, I should be satisfied. My Happiness might come before that time, or it might not. I should be satisfied. I should know that my life was out of my hands. I should know, above all, that my long, long, old, old pain of loneliness would stop, June twenty-seventh, 1903.

I shall die naturally some day—probably after I have grown old and sour. If I have had my Happiness for a year or a day, well and good. I shall be content to grow as old and as sour as the Devil wills. But having had no Happiness—if I find myself growing old and still no Happiness—oh, then I vow I will not live another hour, even if dying were rushing headlong to damnation!

I am, do you see, a philosopher and a coward—with the philosophy of cowardice. I squeeze juice also from this fact sometimes—but the juice is not sweet juice.

The Devil—the fascinating man-devil—it may be, is coming, coming, coming.

And meanwhile I go on and on, in the midst of sand and barrenness.

3 FEBRUARY.

THE town of Butte presents a wonderful field to a student of humanity and human nature. There are not a great many people—seventy thousand perhaps—but those seventy thousand are in their way unparalleled. For mixture, for miscellany—variedness, Bohemianism-where is Butte's rival?

The population is not only of all nationalities and stations, but the nationalities and stations mix and mingle promiscuously with each other, and are partly concealed and partly revealed in the mazes of a veneer that belongs neither to nation nor to station, but to Butte.

The nationalities are many, it is true, but Irish and Cornish predominate. My acquaintance extends widely among the inhabitants of Butte. Sometimes when I feel in the mood for it I spend an afternoon in visiting about among divers curious people.

At some Fourth of July demonstration, or on a Miners' Union day, the heterogeneous herd turns out—and I turn out, with the herd and of it, and meditate and look on. There are Irishmen—Kelleys, Caseys, Calahans, staggering under the weight of much whiskey, shouting out their green-isle maxims; there is the festive Cornishman, ogling and leering, greeting his fellow-countrymen with alcoholic heartiness, and gazing after every feminine creature with lustful eyes; there are Irish women swearing genially at each other in shrill pleasantry, and five or six loudly-vociferous children for each; there are round-faced Cornish women likewise, each with her train of children; there are suave, sleek sporting men just out of the bath-tub; insignificant lawyers, dentists, messenger-boys; "plungers" without number; greasy Italians from Meaderville; greasier French people from the Boulevarde Addition; ancient miners—each of whom was the first to stake a claim in Butte; starved-looking Chinamen here and there; a contingent of Finns and Swedes and Germans; musty, stuffy old Jew pawn-brokers who have crawled out of their holes for a brief recreation; dirt-encrusted Indians and squaws in dirty, gay blankets, from their flea-haunted camp below the town; "box-rustlers"—who are as common in Butte as bar-maids in Ireland; swell, flashy-looking Africans; respectable women with white aprons tied around their waists and sailor-hats on their heads, who have left the children at home and stepped out to see what was going on; innumerable stray youngsters from the dark haunts of Dublin Gulch; heavy restaurant-keepers with toothpicks in their mouths; a vast army of dry-goods clerks—the "paper-collared" gentry; miners of every description; representatives from Dog Town, Chicken Flats, Busterville, Butchertown, and Seldom Seen—suburbs of Butte; pale, thin individuals who sing and dance in beer-halls; smart society people in high traps and tally-hos; impossible women—so-called (though in Butte no one is more possible), in vast hats and extremely plaid stockings; persons who take things seriously and play the races for a living; "beer-jerkers"; "biscuit-shooters"; soft-voiced Mexicans and Arabians;—the dregs, the elite, the humbly respectable, the off-scouring—all thrown together, and shaken up, and mixed well.

One may notice many odd bits of irony as one walks among these. One may notice that the Irishmen are singularly carefree and strong and comfortable—and so jolly! while the Irish women are frumpish and careworn and borne earthward with children. The Cornishman who has consumed the greatest amount of whiskey is the most agreeable, and less and less inclined to leer and ogle. The Cornish woman whose profanity is the shrillest and most genial and voluble, is she whose life seems the most weighted and downtrodden. The young women whose bodies are encased in the tightest and stiffest corsets are in the most wildly hilarious spirits of all. The filthy little Irish youngsters from Dublin Gulch are much brighter and more clever in every way than the ordinary American children who are less filthy. A delicate aroma of cocktails and whiskey-and-soda hangs over even the four-in-hands and automobiles of the upper crust. Gamblers, newsboys, and Chinamen are the most chivalrously courteous among them. And the modest-looking "plunger" who has drunk the greatest number of high-balls is the most gravely, quietly polite of all. The rolling, rollicking, musical profanity of the "ould sod"—Bantry Bay, Donegal, Tyrone, Tipperary—falls much less limpidly from the cigaretted lips of the ten-year-old lad than from those of his mother, who taught it to him. One may notice that the husband and wife who smile the sweetest at each other in the sight of the multitudes are they whose countenances bear various scars and scratches commemorating late evening orgies at home; that the peculiar solid, block-shaped appearance of some of the miners' wives is due quite as much to the quantity of beer they drink as to their annual maternity; that the one grand ruling passion of some men's lives is curiosity;—that the entire herd is warped, distorted, barren, having lived its life in smoke-cured Butte.

A single street in Butte contains people in nearly every walk of life—living side by side resignedly, if not in peace.

In a row of five or six houses there will be living miners and their families, the children of which prevent life from stagnating in the street while their mothers talk to each other—with the inevitable profanity—over the backfences. On the corner above there will be a mysterious widow with one child, who has suddenly alighted upon the neighborhood, stealthily in the night, and is to be seen at rare intervals emerging from her door—the target for dozens of pairs of eager eyes and half as many eager tongues. And when the mysterious widow, with her one child, disappears some night as suddenly and as stealthily as she appeared, an outburst of highly-colored rumors is tossed with astonishing glibness over the various back-fences—all relating to the mysterious widow's shady antecedents and past history, to those of her child, and to the cause of her sudden departure,—no two of which rumors agree in any particular. Across on the opposite corner there will be a company of strange people who also descended suddenly, and upon whom the eyes of the entire block are turned with absorbing interest. They consist of half-a-dozen men and women seemingly bound together only by ties of conviviality. The house is kept closely-blinded and quiet all day, only to burst forth in a blaze of revel in the evening, which revel lasts all night. This goes on until some momentous night, at the request of certain proper ones, a police officer glides quietly into the midst of a scene of unusual gaiety—and the festive company melts into oblivion, never to return. They also are then discussed with rapturous relish and in tones properly lowered, over the back-fences. Farther down the street there will live an interesting being of feminine persuasion who has had five divorces and is in course of obtaining another. These divorces, the causes therefor, the justice thereof, and the future prospects of the multi-grass widow, are gone over, in all their bearings, by the indefatigable tongues. Every incident in the history of the street is put through a course of sprouts by these same tireless members. The Jewish family that lives in the poorest house in the neighborhood, and that is said to count its money by the hundred thousands; the aristocratic family with the Irish-point curtains in the windows—that lives on the county; the family whose husband and father gains for it a comfortable livelihood—forging checks; the miner's family whose wife and mother wastes its substance in diamonds and sealskin coats and other riotous living; the family in extremely straitened circumstances into which new babies arrive in great and distressing numbers; the strange lady with an apoplectic complexion and a wonderfully foul and violent flow of invective—all are discussed over and over and over again. No one is omitted.

And so this is Butte, the promiscuous—the Bohemian. And all these are the Devil's playthings. They amuse him, doubtless.

Butte is a place of sand and barrenness.

The souls of these people are dumb.

4 FEBRUARY.

ALWAYS I wonder, when I die will there be any one to remember me with love?

I know I am not lovable.

That I want it so much only makes me less lovable, it seems. But—who knows?—it may be there will be some one.

My anemone lady does not love me. How can she—since she does not understand me? But she allows me to love her—and that carries me a long way. There are many—oh, a great many—who will not allow you to love them if you would.

There is no one to love me now.

Always I wonder how it will be after some long years when I find myself about to die.

7 FEBRUARY.

IN THIS house where I drag out my accursed, devilish, weary existence, upstairs in the bathroom, on the little ledge at the top of the wainscoting, there are six tooth-brushes: an ordinary white bone-handled one that is my younger brother's; a white twisted-handled one that is my sister's; a flat-handled one that is my older brother's; a celluloid-handled one that is my stepfather's; a silver-handled one that is mine; and another ordinary one that is my mother's. The sight of these tooth-brushes day after day, week after week, and always, is one of the most crushingly maddening circumstances in my fool's life.

Every Friday I wash up the bathroom. Usually I like to do this. I like the feeling of the water squeezing through my fingers, and always it leaves my nails beautifully neat. But the obviousness of those six tooth-brushes signifying me and the five other members of this family and the aimless emptiness of my existence here—Friday after Friday—makes my soul weary and my heart sick.

Never does the pitiable, barren, contemptible, damnable, narrow Nothingness of my life in this house come upon me with so intense a force as when my eyes happen upon those six tooth-brushes.

Among the horrors of the Inquisition, a minute refinement of cruelty was reached when the victim's head was placed beneath a never-ceasing falling of water, drop by drop.

A convict sentenced to solitary confinement, spending his endless days staring at four blank walls, feels that had he committed every known crime he could not possibly deserve his punishment.

I am not undergoing an Inquisition, nor am I a convict in solitary confinement. But I live in a house with people who affect me mostly through their tooth-brushes—and those I should like, above all things, to gather up and pitch out of the bathroom window—and oh, damn them, *damn* them!

You who read this, can you understand the depth of bitterness and hatred that is contained in this for me? Perhaps you can a little if you are a woman and have felt yourself alone.

When I look at the six tooth-brushes a fierce, lurid storm of rage and passion comes over me. Two heavy leaden hands lay hold of my life and press, press, press. They strike the sick, sick weariness to my inmost soul.

Oh, to leave this house and these people, and this intense Nothingness—oh, to pass out from them, forever! But where can I go, what can I do? I feel with mad fury that I am helpless. The grasp of the stepfather and the mother is contemptible and absurd—but with the persistence and tenacity of narrow minds. It is like the two heavy leaden hands. It is not seen—it is not tangible. It is felt.

Once I took away my own silver-handled tooth-brush from the bathroom ledge, and kept it in my bedroom for a day or two. I thought to lessen the effect of the six.

I put it back in the bathroom.

The absence of one accentuated the significant damnation of the others. There was something more forcibly maddening in the five than in the six tooth-brushes. The damnation was not worse, but it developed my feeling about them more vividly.

And so I put my tooth-brush back in the bathroom.

This house is comfortably furnished. My mother spends her life in the adornment of it. The small square rooms are distinctly pretty.

But when I look at them seeingly I think of the proverb

about the dinner of stalled ox.

Yet there is no hatred here, except mine and my bitterness. I am the only one of them whose bitter spirit cries out against things.

But there is that which is subtler and strikes deeper. There is the lack of sympathy—the lack of everything that counts: there is the great, deep Nothing.

How much better were there hatred here than Nothing!

I long hopelessly for will-power, resolution to take my life into my own hands, to walk away from this house some day and never return. I have nowhere to go—no money, and I know the world quite too well to put the slightest faith in its voluntary kindness of heart. But how much better and wider, less damned, less maddening, to go out into it and be beaten and cheated and fooled with, than this!—this thing that gathers itself easily into a circle made of six tooth-brushes with a sufficiency of surplus damnation.

I have read about a woman who went down from Jerusalem to Jericho and fell among thieves. Perhaps she had a house at Jerusalem with six tooth-brushes and Nothingness. In that case she might have rushed gladly into the arms of thieves.

I think of crimes that strike horror and revulsion to my maid-senses. And I think of my Nothingness, and I ask myself were it not better to walk the earth an outcast, a solitary woman, and meet and face even these, than that each and every one of my woman-senses should wear slowly, painfully to shreds, and strain and break—in this unnamable Nothing?

Oh, the dreariness—the hopelessness of Nothing!

There are no words to tell it. And things are always hardest to bear when there are no words for them.

However great one's gift of language may be, there is always something that one can not tell.

I am weary of self—always self. But it must be so.

My life is filled with *self.*

If my soul could awaken fully perhaps I might be lifted out of myself—surely I should be. But my soul is not awake. It is awakening, trying to open its eyes; and it is crying out blindly after something, but it can not know. I have a dreadful feeling that it will stay always like this.

Oh, I feel everything—everything! I feel what might be. And there is Nothing. There are six tooth-brushes.

Would I stop for a few fine distinctions, a theory, a natural law even, to escape from this into Happiness—or into something greatly less?

Misery—misery! If only I could feel it less!

Oh, the weariness, the weariness—as I await the Devil's coming.

8 FEBRUARY.

OFTEN I walk out to a place on the flat valley, below the town, to flirt with Death. There is within me a latent spirit of coquetry, it appears.

Down on the flat there is a certain deep, dark hole with several feet of water at the bottom.

This hole completely fascinates me. Sometimes when I start out to walk in a quite different direction, I feel impelled almost irresistibly to turn and go down on the flat in the direction of the fascinating, deep black hole.

And here I flirt with Death. The hole is so narrow—only about four feet across—and so dark, and so deep! I don't know whether it was intended to be a well, or whether it is an abandoned shaft of some miner. At any rate it is isolated and deserted, and it has a rare loving charm for me.

I go there sometimes in the early evening, and kneel on the edge of it and lean over the dark pit, with my hand grasping a wooden stake that is driven into the ground near by. And I drop little stones down and hear them splash hollowly, and it sounds a long way off.

There is something wonderfully soothing, wonderfully comforting to my unrestful, aching wooden heart in the dark mystery of this fascinating hole. Here is the End for me, if I want it—here is the Ceasing, when I want it. And I lean over and smile quietly.

"No flowers," I say softly to myself, "no weeping idiots, no senseless funeral, no oily undertaker fussing over my woman's-body, no useless Christian prayers. Nothing but this deep dark restful grave."

No one would ever find it. It is a mile and a half from any house.

The water—the dark still water at the bottom—would gurgle over me and make an end quietly. Or if I feared there was not enough water, I would bring with me a syringe and some morphine and inject an immense quantity into one white arm, and kneel over the tender darkness until my youth-weary, waiting-worn senses should be overcome, and my slim, light body should fall. It would splash into the water at the bottom—it would follow the little stones at last. And the black, muddy water would soak in and begin the destroying of my body, and murky bubbles would rise so long as my lungs continued to breathe. Or perhaps my body would fall against the side of the hole, and the head would be against it out of the water. Or perhaps only the face would be out of the water, turned upward to the light above—or turned half-down, and the hair would be darkly wet and heavy, and the face would be blue-white below it, and the eyes would sink inward.

"The End, the End!" I say softly and ecstatically. Yet I do not lean farther out. My hand does not loosen its tight grasp on the wooden stake. I am only flirting with Death now.

Death is fascinating—almost like the Devil. Death makes use of all his arts and wiles, powerful and alluring, and flirts with deadly temptation for me. And I make use of my arts and wiles and tempt him.

Death would like dearly to have me, and I would like dearly to have him. It is a flirtation that has its source in mutual desire. We do not love each other, Death and I,—we are not friends. But we desire each other sensually, lustfully.

Sometime I suppose I shall yield to the desire. I merely play at it now—but in an unmistakable manner. Death knows it is only a question of time.

But first the Devil must come. First the Devil, then Death: a deep dark soothing grave—and the early evening, "and a little folding of the hands to sleep."

12 FEBRUARY.

I AM in no small degree, I find, a sham—a player to the gallery. Possibly this may be felt as you read these analyses.

While all of these emotions are written in the utmost seriousness and sincerity, and are exactly as I feel them, day after day—so far as I have the power to express what I feel—still I aim to convey through them all the idea that I am lacking in the grand element of Truth—that there is in the warp and woof of my life a thread that is false—false.

I don't know how to say this without the fear of being misunderstood. When I say I am in a way a sham, I have no reference to the truths as I have given them in this Portrayal, but to a very light and subtle thing that runs through them.

Oh, do not think for an instant that this analysis of my emotions is not perfectly sincere and real, and that I have not felt all of them more than I can put into words. They are my tears—my life-blood!

But in my life, in my personality, there is an essence of falseness and insincerity. A thin, fine vapor of fraud hangs always over me and dampens and injures some things in me that I value.

I have not succeeded thoroughly in analyzing this—it is so thin, so elusive, so faint—and yet not little. It is a natural thing enough viewed in the light of my other traits.

I have lived my nineteen years buried in an environment at utter variance with my natural instincts, where my inner life is never touched, and my sympathies very rarely, if ever, appealed to. I never disclose my real desires or the texture of my soul. Never, that is to say, to any one except my one friend, the anemone lady.—And so every day of my life I am playing a part; I am keeping an immense bundle of things hidden under my cloak. When one has played a part—a false part—all one's life, for I was a sly, artful little liar even in the days of five and six; then one is marked. One may never rid oneself of the mantle of falseness, charlatanry—particularly if one is innately a liar.

A year ago when the friendship of my anemone lady was given me, and she would sometimes hear sympathetically some long-silent bit of pain, I felt a snapping of tense-drawn cords, a breaking away of flood-gates—and a strange, new pain. I felt as if I must clasp her gentle hand tightly and give way to the pent-up, surging tears of eighteen years. I had wanted this tender thing more than anything else all my life, and it was given me suddenly.

I felt a convulsion and a melting, within.

But I could not tell my one friend exactly what I felt. There was no doubt in my own mind as to my own perfect sincerity of feeling, but there was with it and around it this vapor of fraud, a spirit of falseness that rose and confronted me and said, "hypocrite," "fool."

It may be that the spirit of falseness is itself a false thing,—yet true or false, it is with me always. I have tried, in writing out my emotions, to convey an idea of this sham element while still telling everything faithfully true. Sometimes I think I have succeeded, and at other times I seem to have signally failed. This element of falseness is absolutely the very thinnest, the very finest, the rarest of all the things in my many-sided character.

It is not the most unimportant.

I have seen visions of myself walking in various pathways. I have seen myself trying one pathway and another. And always it is the same: I see before me in the path, darkening the way and filling me with dread and discouragement, a great black shadow—the shadow of my own element of falseness.

I can not rid myself of it.

I am an innate liar.

This is a hard thing to write about. Of all things it is the most liable to be misunderstood. You will probably misunderstand it, for I have not succeeded in giving the right idea of it. I aimed at it and missed it. It eluded me completely.

You must take the idea as I have just now presented it for what it may be worth. This is as near as I can come to it. But it is something infinitely finer and rarer.

It is a difficult task to show to others a thing which, though I feel and recognize it thoroughly, I have not yet analyzed for myself.

But this is a complete Portrayal of me—as I await the Devil's coming—and I must tell everything—everything.

13 FEBRUARY.

SO THEN, yes. As I have said, I find that I am quite, quite odd. My various acquaintances say that I am funny. They say, "Oh, it's that Mary MacLane, Dolly's younger sister. She's funny." But I call it oddity. I bear the hall-mark of oddity.

There was a time, a year or two since, when I was an exceedingly sensitive little fool—sensitive in that it used to strike very deep when my young acquaintances would call me funny and find in me a vent for their distinctly unfriendly ridicule. My years in the high school were not years of joy. Two years ago I had not yet risen above these things. I was a sensitive little fool.

But that sensitiveness, I rejoice to say, has gone from me. The opinion of these young people, or of these old people, is now a thing that is quite unable to affect me.

The more I see of conventionality, it seems, the more I am odd.

Though I am voting and feminine—very feminine—yet I am not that quaint conceit, a *girl*: the sort of person that Laura E. Richards writes about, and Nora Perry, and Louisa M. Alcott—girls with bright eyes, and with charming faces (they always have charming faces), standing with reluctant feet where the brook and river meet,—and all that sort of thing.

I missed all that.

I have read some girl-books, a few years ago—*Hildegarde Grahame* and *What Katy Did*, and all—but I read them from afar. I looked at those creatures from behind a high board fence. I felt as if I had more tastes in common with the Jews wandering through the wilderness, or with a band of fighting Amazons. I am not a girl. I am a woman, of a kind. I began to be a woman at twelve, or more properly, a genius.

And then, usually, if one is not a girl one is a heroine—of the kind you read about. But I am not a heroine, either. A heroine is beautiful—eyes like the sea shoot opaque glances from under drooping lids—walks with undulating movements, her bright smile haunts one still, falls methodically in love with a man—always with a man, eats things (they are always called "viands") with a delicate appetite, and on special occasions her voice is full of tears. I do none of these things. I am not beautiful. I do not walk with undulating movements—indeed, I have never seen any one walk so, except, perhaps, a cow that has been overfed. My bright smile haunts no one. I shoot no opaque glances from my eyes, which are not like the sea by any means. I have never eaten any viands, and my appetite for what I do eat is most excellent. And my voice has never yet, to my knowledge, been full of tears.

No, I am not a heroine.

There never seem to be any plain heroines, except Jane Eyre, and she was very unsatisfactory. She should have entered into marriage with her beloved Rochester in the first place. I should have, let there be a dozen mad wives upstairs. But I suppose the author thought she must give her heroine some desirable thing—high moral principles, since she was not beautiful. Some people say that beauty is a curse. It may be true, but I'm sure I should not have at all minded being cursed a little. And I know several persons who might say the same. But, anyway, I wish some one would write a book about a plain, bad heroine so that I might feel in real sympathy with her.

So far from being a girl or a heroine, I am a thief—as I have before suggested.

I mind me of how, not long since, I stole three dollars. A woman whom I know rather well, and lives near, called me into her house as I was passing and asked me to do an errand for her. She was having an ornate gown made, and she needed some more applique with which to festoon it. The applique cost nine dollars a yard. My trusting neighbor gave me a bit of the braid for a sample and two twenty-dollar bills. I was to get four yards. I did so, and came back and gave her the braid and a single dollar. The other three dollars I kept myself. I wanted three dollars very much, to put with a few that I already had in my purse. My trusting neighbor is of the kind that throws money about carelessly. I knew she would not pay any attention to a little detail like that,—she was deeply interested in her new frock; or perhaps she would think I had got thirty-nine dollars' worth of applique. At any rate, she did not need the money, and I wanted three dollars, and so I stole it.

I am a thief.

It has been suggested to me that I am a kleptomaniac. But I am sure my mind is perfectly sane. I have no such excuse. I am a plain, downright thief.

This is only one of my many peculations. I steal money, or anything that I want, whenever I can, nearly always. It amuses me—and one must be amused.

I have only two stipulations: that the person to whom it belongs does not need it pressingly, and that there is not the smallest chance of being found out. (And of course I could not think of stealing from my one friend.)

It would be extremely inconvenient to be known as a thief, merely.

When the world knows you are a thief it blinds itself completely to your other attributes. It calls you a thief, and there's an end. I am a genius as well as a thief—but the world would quite overlook that fact. "A thief's a thief," says the world. That is very true. But the mere fact of being a thief should not exclude the consideration of one's other traits. When the world knows you are a Methodist minister, for instance, it will admit that you may also be a violinist, or a chemist, or a poet, and will credit you therefor. And so if it condemns you for being a thief, it should at the same time admire you for being a genius. If it does not admire you for being a genius, then it has no right to condemn you for being a thief.

—And why the world should condemn any one for being a thief—when there is not within its confines any one who is not a thief in some way—is a bit of irony upon which I have wasted much futile logic.—

I am not trying to justify myself for stealing. I do not consider it a thing that needs to be justified, any more than walking or eating or going to bed. But, as I say, if the world knew that I am a thief without being first made aware with emphasis that I am some other things also, then the world would be a shade cooler for me than it already is—which would be very cool indeed.

And so in writing my Portrayal I have dwelt upon other things at some length before touching on my thieving propensities.

None of my acquaintances would suspect that I am a thief. I look so respectable, so refined, so "nice," so inoffensive, so sweet, even!

But, for that matter, I am a great many things that I do not appear to be.

The woman from whom I stole the three dollars, if she reads this, will recognize it. This will be inconvenient. I fervently hope she may not read it. It is true she is not of the kind that reads.

But, after all, it's of no consequence. This Portrayal is Mary MacLane: her wooden heart, her young woman's-body, her mind, her soul.

The world may run and read.

I will tell you what I did with the three dollars. In Dublin Gulch, which is a rough quarter of Butte inhabited by poor Irish people, there lives an old world-soured, wrinkled-faced woman. She lives alone in a small, untidy house. She swears frightfully like a parrot, and her reputation is bad—so bad, indeed, that even the old woman's compatriots in Dublin Gulch do not visit her lest they damage their own. It is true that the profane old woman's morals are not good—have never been good—judged by the world's standards. She bears various marks of cold, rough handling on her mind and body. Her life has all but run its course. She is worn out.

Once in a while I go to visit this old woman—my reputation must be sadly damaged by now.

I sit with her for an hour or two and listen to her. She is extremely glad to have me there. Except me she has no one to talk to but the milkman, the groceryman, and the butcher. So always she is glad to see me. There is a certain bond of sympathy between her and me. We are fond of each other. When she sees me picking my way towards her house, her hard, sour face softens wonderfully and a light of distinct friendliness comes into her green eyes.

Don't you know, there are few people enough in the world whose hard, sour faces will soften at sight of you and a distinctly friendly light come into their green eyes. For myself, I find such people few indeed.

So the profane old woman and I are fond of each other. No question of morals, or of immorals, comes between us. We are equals.

I talk to her a little—but mostly she talks. She tells me of the time when she lived in County Galway, when she was young—and of her several husbands, and of some who were not husbands, and of her children scattered over the earth. And she shows me old tin-types of these people. She has told me the varied tale of her life a great many times. I like to hear her tell it. It is like nothing else I have heard. The story in its unblushing simplicity, the sour-faced old woman sitting telling it, and the tin-types,—contain a thing that is absurdly, grotesquely, tearlessly sad.

Once when I went to her house I brought with me six immense, heavy, fragrant chrysanthemums.

They had been bought with the three dollars I had stolen.

It pleased me to buy them for the profane old woman. They pleased her also—not because she cares much for flowers, but because I brought them to her. I knew they would please her, but that was not the reason I gave her them.

I did it purely and simply to please myself.

I knew the profane old woman would not be at all concerned as to whether they had been bought with stolen money or not, and my only regret was that I had not had an opportunity to steal a larger sum so that I might have bought more chrysanthemums without inconveniencing my purse.

But as it was they filled her dirty little dwelling with perfume and color.

Long ago, when I was six, I was a thief—only I was not then, as now, a graceful, light-fingered thief—I had not the philosophy of stealing.

When I would steal a copper cent out of my mother's pocketbook I would feel a dreadful, suffocating sinking in my bad heart, and for days and nights afterwards—long after I had eaten the chocolate mouse—the copper cent would haunt me and haunt me, and oh, how I wished it back in that pocketbook with the clasp shut tight and the bureau drawer locked!

And so, is it not finer to be nineteen and a thief, with the philosophy of stealing—than to be six and haunted day and night by a copper cent?

For now always my only regret is, when I have stolen five dollars, that I did not steal ten while I was about it.

It is a long time ago since I was six.

17 February.

TODAY I walked over the hill where the sun vanishes down in the afternoon.

I followed the sun so far as I could, but two even very good legs can do no more than carry one into the midst of the sunshine—and then one may stand and take leave, lovingly, of it.

I stood in the valley below the hill and looked away at the gold-yellow mountains that rise into the cloudy blue, and at the long gray stretches of rolling sand. It all reminded me of the Devil and the Happiness he will bring me.

Some day the Devil will come to me and say: "Come with me."

And I will answer: "Yes."

And he will take me away with him to a place where it is wet and green—where the yellow, yellow sunshine falls on heaven-kissing hills, and misty, cloudy masses float over the valleys.

And for days I shall be happy—happy—happy!

For *days!* The Devil and I will love each other intensely, perfectly—for days! He will be incarnate, but he will not be a man. He will be the man-devil, and his soul will take mine to itself and they will be one—for days.

Imagine me raised out of my misery and obscurity, dullness and Nothingness, into the full, brilliant life of the Devil—for days!

The love of the man-devil will enter into my barren, barren life and melt all the cold, hard things, and water the barrenness, and a million little green growing plants will start out of it; and a clear, sparkling spring will flow over it—through the dreary, sandy stretches of my bitterness, among the false stony roadways of my pain and hatred. And a great rushing, flashing cataract of melting love will flow over my weariness and unrest and wash it away forever. My soul will be fully awakened and there will be a million little sweet new souls in the green growing things. And they will fill my life with everything that is beautiful—tenderness, and divineness, and compassion, and exaltation, and uplifting grace, and light, and rest, and gentleness, and triumph, and truth, and peace. My life will be borne far out of self, and self will sink quietly out of sight—and I shall see it farther and farther away, until it disappears.

"It is the last—the *last*—of that Mary MacLane," I will say, and I will feel a long, sighing, quivering farewell.

A thousand years of misery—and now a million years of Happiness.

When the sun is setting in the valley and the crests of those heaven-kissing hills are painted violet and purple, and the valley itself is reeking and swimming in yellow-gold light, the man-devil—whom I love more than all—and I will go out into it.

We will be saturated in the yellow light of the sun and the gold light of Love.

The man-devil will say to me: "Look, you little creature, at this beautiful picture of joy and Happiness. It is the picture of your life as it will be while I am with you—and I am with you for days."

Ah, yes, I will take a last, long farewell of this Mary MacLane. Not one faint shadow of her weary wretched Nothingness will remain.

There will be instead a brilliant, buoyant, joyous creature—transformed, adorned, garlanded by the love of the Devil.

My mind will be a treasure-house of art, swept and garnished and strong and at its best.

My barren, hungry heart will come at last to its own. The red flames of the man-devil's love will burn out forever its pitiable, distorted, wooden quality, and he will take it and cherish it—and give me his.

My young woman's-body likewise will be metamorphosed, and I shall feel it developing and filled with myriads of little contentments and pleasures. Always my young woman's-body is a great and important part of me, and when I am married to the Devil its finely-organized nerve-power and intricate sensibility will be culminated to marvelous completeness. My soul—upon my soul will descend consciously the light that never was on land or sea.

This will be for days—for days.

No matter what came before, I will say; no matter what comes afterward. just now it is the man-devil, my best-beloved, and I, living in the yellow light.

Think of living with the Devil in a bare little house, in the midst of green wetness and sweetness and yellow light—for days!

In the gray dawn it will be ineffably sweet and beautiful, with shining leaves and the gray, unfathomable air, and the wet grass, and all.

"Be happy now, my weary little wife," the Devil will say.

And the long, long yellow-gold day will be filled with the music of Real Life.

My grandest possibility will be realized. The world contains a great many things—and this is my grandest possibility realized!

I will weep rapturous tears.

When I think of all this and write it there is in me a feeling that is more than pain.

Perhaps the very sweetest, the tenderest, the most pitiful and benign human voice in the world could sing these things and this feeling set to their own wondrous music,—and it would echo far—far,—and you would understand.

20 FEBRUARY.

AT TIMES when I walk among the natural things—the barren, natural things—I know that I believe in Something. Why can I not call it God and pray to it?

There is Something—I do not know it intellectually, but I feel it—I feel it—with my soul. It does not seem to reach down to me. It does not pity me. It does not look at me tenderly in my unhappiness.

My soul feels only that it is there.

No. It is not all-loving, all-gracious, all-pitying. It hurts me—it hurts me always as I walk over the sand. But even while it hurts me it seems to promise—ah, those beautiful things that it promises me!

And then the hurting is anguish—for I know that the promises will never be fulfilled.

There is within me a thing that is aching, aching, aching always as the days pass.

It is not my pain of wanting, nor my pain of unrest, nor my pain of bitterness, nor of hatred. I know those in all their own anguish.

This aching is another pain. It is a pain that I do not know—that I feel ignorantly but sharply, and, Oh, it is torture, torture!

My soul is worn and weary with pain. There is no compassion—no mercy upon me. There is no one to help me bear it. It is just I alone out on the sand and barrenness. It is cruel anguish to be always alone—and so long—oh, so long!

Nineteen years are as ages to you when you are nineteen.

When you are nineteen there is no experience to tell you that all things have an end.

This aching pain has no end.

I feel no tears now, but I feel heavy sobs that shake my life to its center.

My soul is wandering in a wilderness.

There is a great light sometimes that draws my soul toward it. When my soul turns toward it, it shines out brilliant and dazzling and awful—and the worn, sensitive thing shrinks away, and shivers, and is faint.

Shall my soul have to know this Light, inevitably? Must it, some day, plunge into this?

Oh, it may be—it may be. But I know that I shall die with the pain.

There are times when the great Light is dim and beautiful as the starlight—the utter agony of it—the cruel, ineffable loveliness!

Do you understand this ? I am telling you my young passionate life-agony? Do you listen to it indifferently? Has it no meaning for any one? For me it means everything. For me it makes life old, long, weariness.

It may be that you know. And perhaps you would even weep a little with me if you had time.

It is as if this Light were the light of the Christian religion—and the Christian religion is full of hatred. It says, "Come unto me, you that are heavy laden, and I will give you rest." But when you would go, when you reach up with your weary hands, it sends you a too-brilliant Light—it makes you fair, wondrous promises—it puts you off. You beseech it in your suffering—

> *While the waters near me roll,*
> *While the tempest still is high—*

but it does not listen—it does not care. Worship me, worship me, it says, but after that let me alone. There is a bookful of promises. Take it and thank me and worship me.

It does not care.

If I obey it, it looks on indifferently. If I disobey it, it looks on indifferently. If I am in woe, it looks on indifferently. If I am in a brief joy, it looks on indifferently.

I am left all alone—all alone.

The Light is shown me and I reach after it, but it is placed high out of my reach.

I see the promises in the Light. Oh, why—*why* does it promise these things! Is not the burden of life already greater than I can bear? And there is the story of the Christ. It is beautiful. It is damningly beautiful. It draws the tears of pain and soft anguish from me at the sense of beauty. And when every nerve in me is melted and overflowing, then suddenly I am conscious that it is a lie—a *lie*.

Everywhere I turn there is Nothing—Nothing.

My soul wails out its grief in loneliness.

My soul wanders hither and thither in the dark wilderness and asks, asks always in blind, dull agony, How long?—how long?

22 FEBRUARY.

LIFE is a pitiful thing.

I STAND in the midst of my sand and barrenness and gaze hard at everything that is within my range of vision—and ruin my eyes trying to see into the darkness beyond.

And nearly always I feel a vague contempt for you, fine, brave world—for you and all the things that I see from my barrenness. But I promise you, if some one comes from among you over the sunset hill one day with love for me, I will fall at your feet.

I am a selfish, conceited, impudent little animal, it is true, but, after all, I am only one grand conglomeration of Wanting—and when some one comes over the barren hill to satisfy the wanting. I will be humble, humble in my triumph.

It is a difficult thing—a most difficult thing—to live on as one year follows another, from childhood slowly to womanhood, without one single sharer of your life—to be alone, always alone, when your one friend is gone. Oh, yes, it is hard! Particularly when one is not high-minded and spiritual, when one's near longing is not a God and a religion, when one wants above all things the love of a human being—when one is a woman, young and all alone. Doubtless you know this. After all, fine brave world, there are some things that you know very well. Whether or not you care, a quite different matter.

You have the power to take this wooden heart in a tight, suffocating grasp. You have the power to do this with pain for me, and you have the power to do it with ravishing gentleness. But whether or not you will is another matter.

You may think evil of me before you have finished reading this. You will be very right to think so—according to your standards. But sometimes you see evil where there is no evil, and think evil when the only evil is in your own brains.

My life is a dry and barren life. You can change it.

Oh, the little more, and how much it is
And the little less, and what worlds away.

Yes, you can change it. Stranger things have happened. Again, whether you will—that is a quite different thing.

No doubt you are the People and wisdom will die with

you. I do not question that. I will admit and believe anything you may assert about yourselves. I do not want your wisdom, your judgment. I want some one to come up over the barren sunset hill. My thoughts are the thoughts of youth, which are said to be long, long thoughts.

Your life is multi-colored and filled with people. My life is of the gray of sand and barrenness, and consists of Mary MacLane, the longing for Happiness, and the memory of the anemone lady.

This Portrayal is my deepest sincerity, my tears, my drops of red blood. Some of it is wrung from me—wrung by my ambition to tell everything. It is not altogether good that I should give you all this, since I do not give it for love of you. I am giving it in exchange for a few gayly-colored things. I want you to know all these passions and emotions. I give them with the utmost freedom. I shall be furious indeed if you do not take them. At the same time, the fact that I am exchanging my tears and my drops of red blood for your gayly-colored trifles is not a thing that thrills me with delight.

But it's of little moment. When the Devil comes over the hill with Happiness I will rush at him frantically headlong—and nothing else will matter.

25 February.

MARY MACLANE—what are you, you forlorn, desolate little creature? Why are you not of and in the galloping herd? Why is it that you stand out separate against the background of a gloomy sky? Why can you not enter into the lives and sympathies of other young creatures? There have been times when you strained every despairing nerve to do so—before you realized that these things were not for you, that the only sympathy for you was that of Mary MacLane, and the only things for you were those you could take yourself—not which were given you. And your things are few, few, you starved, lean little mud-cat—you worn, youth-weary, obscure little genius!

Oh, it is a wearisome waiting—for the Devil.

28 FEBRUARY.

TODAY when I walked over my sand and barrenness I felt Infinite Grief.

Everything is beyond me.

Nothing is mine.

My single friendship shines brightly before me, and is fascinating—and always just out of my reach.

I want the love and sympathy of human beings, and I repel human beings.

Yes, I repel human beings.

There is something about me that faintly and finely and unmistakably repels.

When my Happiness comes, shall I be able to have it? Shall I ever have anything?

This repellent power is not an outward quality. It is something that comes from deeply, deeply within. It is something that was there in the Beginning. It is a thing from the Original.

There is no ridding myself of it. There is no ridding myself of it. There is no ridding myself of it.

Oh, I am damned—damned!

There is not one soul in the world to feel for me and with me—not one out of all the millions. No one can understand—*no one*.

You are saying to yourself that I imagine this.

What right have you to say so? You don't know anything about me. I know all about me. I studied all the elements and phases in my life for years and years. I do not imagine anything. I am even fool enough to shut my eyes to some things until, inevitably, I know I must meet them. I am racked with the passions of youth, and I am young in years. Beyond that I am mature—old. I am not a child in anything but my passions and my years. I feel and recognize everything thoroughly. I have not to imagine anything. My inner life is before my eyes.

There is something about me that no one can understand. Can there ever be any one to understand? Shall I not always walk my barren road alone?

This follows me incessantly. It is burning like a smouldering fire every hour of my life.

Oh, deep black Despair!
How I suffer, how I suffer—just in being alive.
I feel Infinite Grief.
Oh, Infinite Grief—

2 MARCH.

OFTEN in the early morning I leave my bed and get me dressed and go out into the Gray Dawn. There is something about the Gray Dawn that makes me wish the world would stop, that the sun would never more come up over the edge, that my life would go on and on and rest in the Gray Dawn.

In the Gray Dawn every hard thing is hidden by a gray mantle of charity, and only the light, vague, caressing fancies are left.

Sometimes I think I am a strange, strange creature—something not of earth, nor yet of heaven, nor of hell. I think at times I am a little thing fallen on the earth by mistake: a thing thrown among foreign, unfitting elements, where there is nothing in touch with it, where life is a continual struggle, where every little door is closed—every Why unanswered, and itself knows not where to lay its head. I feel a deadly certainty in some moments that the wild world contains not one moment of rest for me, that there will never be any rest, that my woman's-soul will go on asking long, long centuries after my woman's-body is laid in its grave.

I felt this in the Gray Dawn this morning, but the gray charitable mantle softened it. Always I feel most acutely in the Gray Dawn, but always there is the thing to soften it.

The gray atmosphere was charged. There was a tense electrical thrill in the cold, soft air. My nerves were keenly alive. But the gray curtain was mercifully there. I did not feel too much.

How I wished the yellow, beautiful sun would never more come up over the edge to show me my nearer anguish!

"Stay with me, stay with me, soft Gray Dawn," implored every one of my tiny lives. "Let me forget. Let the vanity, the pain, the longing sink deep and vanish—all of it, all of it! And let me rest in the midst of the Gray Dawn.

I heard music—the silent music of myriad voices that you hear when all is still. One of them came and whispered to me softly: "Don't suffer any more just now, little Mary MacLane. You suffer enough in the brightness of the sun and the blackness of the night. This is the Gray Dawn. Take a little rest."

"Yes," I said, "I will take a little rest."

And then a wild, swelling chorus of voices whispered in the stillness: "Rest, rest, rest, little Mary MacLane. Suffer in the brightness, suffer in the blackness—your soul, your wooden heart, your woman's-body. But now a little rest—a little rest."

"A little rest," I said again.

And straightway I began resting lest the sun should come too quickly over the edge.

When I have heard in summer the wind in a forest of pines, blowing a wondrous symphony of purity and truth, my varied nature felt itself abashed and there was a sinking in my wooden heart. The beauty of it ravished my senses, but it savored crushingly of the virtue that is far above and beyond me, and I felt a certain sore, despairing grief.

But the Gray Dawn is in perfect sympathy. It is quite as beautiful as the wind in the pines, and its truth and purity are extremely gentle, and partly hidden under the gray curtain.

Almost I can be a different Mary MacLane out in the Gray Dawn. Let me forget all the mingled agonies of my life. Let me walk in the midst of this soft grayness and drink of the waters of Lethe.

The Gray Dawn is not Paradise; it is not a Happy Valley; it is not a Garden of Eden; it is not a Vale of Cashmere. It is the Gray Dawn—soft, charitable, tender. "The brilliant celestial yellow will come soon," it says; "you will suffer then to your greatest extent. But now I am here—and so, rest."

And so in the Gray Dawn I was forgetting for a brief period. I was submerged for a little in Lethe, river of oblivion. If I had seen some one coming over the near horizon with Happiness I should have protested: Wait, wait until the Gray Dawn has passed.

The deep, deep blue of the summer sky stirs me to a half-painful joy. The cool green of a swiftly-flowing river fills my heart with unquiet longings. The red, red of the sunset sky convulses my entire being with passion. But the dear Gray Dawn brings me Rest.

Oh, the Gray Dawn is sweet—sweet!

Could I not die for very love of it!

The Gray Dawn can do no wrong. If those myriad voices suddenly had begun to sing a voluptuous evil song of the so great evil that I could not understand, but that I could feel instantly, still the Gray Dawn would have been fine and sweet and beautiful.

Always I admire Mary MacLane greatly—though sometimes in my admiration I feel a complete contempt for her. But in the Gray Dawn I love Mary MacLane tenderly and passionately.

I seem to take on a strange, calm indifference to everything in the world but just Mary MacLane and the Gray Dawn. We two are identified with each other and joined together in shadowy vagueness from the rest of the world.

As I walked over my sand and barrenness in the Gray Dawn a poem ran continuously through my mind. It expressed to me in my gray condition an ideal life and death and ending. Every desire of my life melted away in the Gray Dawn except one good wish that my own life and death might be short and obscure and complete like them. The poem was this beautiful one of Charles Kingsley's:

Oh, Mary, go and call the cattle home,
And call the cattle home,
And call the cattle home,
Across the sands of Dee!'
The western wind was wild and dank with foam,
And all alone went she.

The creeping tide came up along the sand,
And o'er and o'er the sand,
And round and round the sand,
As far as eye could see;
The blinding mist came up and hid the land—
And never home came she.

Oh, is it weed, or fish, or floating hair?—
A tress of golden hair,
Of drowned maiden's hair,
Above the nets at sea.
Was never salmon yet that shone so fair
Among the stakes on Dee.

They rowed her in across the rolling foam,
The cruel, crawling foam,
The cruel, hungry foam,
To her grave beside the sea;
But still the boatmen hear her call the cattle home
Across the sands of Dee.

This is a poem perfect. And in the Gray Dawn it expresses to me a most desirable thing—a short, eventless life, a sudden ceasing, and a forgotten voice sometimes calling. This Mary, in the Gray Dawn, would wish nothing else. If the waters rolled over me now—over my short, eventless life—there would be the sudden ceasing,—and the anemone lady would hear my voice sometimes, and remember me—the anemone lady and one or two others. And after a short time even my pathetic, passionate voice would sound faint and be forgotten, and my world of sand and barrenness would know me and my weary little life-tragedy no more.

And well for me, I say,—in the Gray Dawn.

It is different—oh, very different—when the yellow bursts through the gray. And the yellow is with me all day long, and at sunset—the red, red line!

Yet—oh, sweet Gray Dawn!

5 March.

SOMETIMES I am seized with nearer, vivider sensations of love for my one friend, the anemone lady.

She is so dear—so beautiful!

My love for her is a peculiar thing. It is not the ordinary woman-love. It is something that burns with a vivid fire of its own. The anemone lady is enshrined in a temple on the inside of my heart that shall always only be hers.

She is my first love—my only dear one.

The thought of her fills me with a multitude of feelings, passionate yet wonderfully tender,—with delight, with rare, undefined emotions, with a suggestion of tears.

Oh, dearest anemone lady, shall I ever be able to forget your beautiful face! There may be some long, crowded years before me; it may be there will be people and people entering and departing—but, oh, no—no, I shall never forget! There will be in my life always—always the faint sweet perfume of the blue anemone: the memory of my one friend.

Before she went away, to see her, to be near her, was an event in my life—a coloring of the dullness. Always when I used to look at her there would rush a train of things over my mind, a vaguely glittering pageant that came only with her, and that held an always-vivid interest for me.

There were manifold and varied treasures in this train. There were skies of spangled sapphire, and there were lilies, and violets wet with dew. There was the music of violins, and wonderful weeds from the deep sea, and songs of troubadours, and gleaming white statues. There were ancient forests of oak and clematis vines; there were lemon-trees, and fretted palaces, and moss-covered old castles with moats and draw-bridges and tiny mullioned windows with diamond panes. There was a cold, glittering cataract of white foam, and a little green boat far off down the river, drifting along under drooping willows. There was a tree of golden apples, and a banquet in a beautiful house with the melting music of lutes and harps, and mulled orange-wine in tall, thin glasses. There was a field of long, fine grass, soft as bat's-wool, and there were birds of brilliant plumage—scarlet and indigo with gold-tipped wings.

All these and a thousand fancies alike vaguely glittering would rush over me when I was with the anemone lady. Always my brain was in a gentle delirium. My nerves were unquiet.

It was because I love her.

Oh, there is not—there can never be—another anemone lady!

My life is a desert—a desert, but the thin, clinging perfume of the blue anemone reaches to its utter confines. And nothing in the desert is the same because of that perfume. Years will not fade the blue of the anemone, nor a thousand bitter winds blow away the rare fragrance.

I feel in the anemone lady a strange attraction of sex. There is in me a masculine element that, when I am thinking of her, arises and overshadows all the others.

"Why am I not a man," I say to the sand and barrenness with a certain strained, tense passion, "that I might give this wonderful, dear, delicious woman an absolutely perfect love!"

And this is my predominating feeling for her.

So then, it is not the woman-love, but the man-love, set in the mysterious sensibilities of my woman-nature. It brings me pain and pleasure mingled in that odd, odd fashion.

Do you think a man is the only creature with whom one may fall in love?

Often I see coming across the desert a long line of light. My soul turns toward it and shrinks away from it as it does from all the lights. Some day, perhaps, all the lights will roll into one terrible white effervescence and rush over my soul and kill it. But this light does not bring so much of pain, for it is soft and silvery, and always with it is the Soul of Anemone.

8 March.

THERE are several things in the world for which I, of womankind and nineteen years, have conceived a forcible repugnance—or rather, the feeling was born in me; I did not have to conceive it.

Often my mind chants a fervent litany of its own that runs somewhat like this:

From women and men who dispense odors of musk; from little boys with long curls; from the kind of people who call a woman's figure her "shape": Kind Devil, deliver me.

From all sweet girls; from "gentlemen"; from feminine men: Kind Devil, deliver me.

From black under-clothing—and any color but white; from hips that wobble as one walks; from persons with fishy eyes; from the books of Archibald C. Gunter and Albert Ross: Kind Devil, deliver me.

From the soft persistent, maddening glances of water-cart drivers: Kind Devil, deliver me.

From lisle-thread stockings; from round, tight garters; from brilliant brass belts: Kind Devil, deliver me.

From insipid sweet wine; from men who wear mustaches; from the sort of people that call legs "limbs"; from bedraggled white petticoats: Kind Devil, deliver me.

From unripe bananas; from bathless people; from a waist-line that slopes up in the front: Kind Devil, deliver me.

From an ordinary man; from a bad stomach, bad eyes, and bad feet: Kind Devil, deliver me.

From red note-paper; from a rhinestone-studded comb in my hair; from weddings: Kind Devil, deliver me.

From cod-fish balls; from fried eggplant, fried beef-steak, fried porkchops, and fried French toast: Kind Devil, deliver me.

From wax flowers off a wedding-cake, under glass; from thin-soled shoes; from tape-worms; from photographs perched up all over my house: Kind Devil, deliver me.

From soft old bachelors and soft old widowers; from any masculine thing that wears a pale blue necktie; from agonizing elocutionists who recite *Curfew Shall Not Ring Tonight*, and *The Lips That Touch Liquor Shall Never Touch Mine*; from a Salvation Army singing hymns in slang: Kind Devil, deliver me.

From people who persist in calling my good body "mere vile clay"; from idiots who appear to know all about me and enjoin me not to bathe my eyes in hot water since it hurts their own; from fools who tell me what I "want" to do: Kind Devil, deliver me.

From a nice young man; from tin spoons; from popular songs: Kind Devil, deliver me.

From pleasant old ladies who tell a great many uninteresting, obvious lies; from men with watch-chains draped across their middles; from some paintings of the old masters which I am unable to appreciate; from side-saddles: Kind Devil, deliver me.

From the kind of man who sings, "Oh, Promise Me!"—who sings *at* it; from constipated dressmakers; from people who don't wash their hair often enough: Kind Devil, deliver me.

From a servant girl with false-teeth; from persons who make a regular practice of rubbing oily mixtures into their faces;

from a bed that sinks in the middle: Kind Devil, deliver me.

And so on and on and on. And in each petition I am deeply sincere. But, kind Devil, only bring me Happiness and I will more than willingly be annoyed by all these things. Happiness for two days, kind Devil, and then, if you will, languishing widowers, lisle-thread stockings—anything, for the rest of my life.

And hurry, kind Devil, pray—for I am weary.

9 MARCH.

IT IS astonishing to me how very many contemptible, petty vanities; are lodged in the crevices of my genius. My genius itself is one grand good vanity—but it is not contemptible. And even those little vanities—though they are contemptible, I do not hold them in contempt by any means. I smile involuntarily at their absurdness sometimes, but I know well that they have their function.

They are peculiarly of my mind, my humanness, and they are useful therein. When this mind stretches out its hand for things and finds only wilderness and Nothingness all about it, and draws the hand back empty, then it can only turn back—like my soul—to itself. And it finds these innumerable little vanities to quiet it and help it. My soul has no vanity, and it has nothing, nothing to quiet it. My soul is wearing itself out, eating itself away. These vanities are a miserable substitute for the rose-colored treasures that it sees a great way off and even imagines in its folly that it may have, if it continues to reach after them. Yet the vanities are something. They prevent my erratic, analytical mind from finding a great Nothing when it turns back upon itself. If I were not so unceasingly engrossed with my sense of misery and loneliness my mind would produce beautiful, wonderful logic: I am a genius—a genius—a genius. Even after all this you may not realize that I am a genius. It is a hard thing to show. But, for myself, I feel it. It is enough for me that I feel it.

I am not a genius because I am foreign to everything in the world, nor because I am intense, nor because I suffer. One may be all of these and yet not have this marvelous perceptive sense. My genius is because of nothing. It was born in me as germs of evil were born in me. And mine is a genius that has been given to no one else. The genius itself enables me to be thoroughly convinced of this.

It is hopeless, never-ending loneliness!

My ancestors in their Highlands—some of them—were endowed with second sight. My genius is not in the least like second sight. That savors of the supernatural, the mysterious. My genius is a sound, sure, earthly sense, with no suggestion of mystery or occultism. It is an inner sense that enables me to feel and know things that I could not possibly put into thought, much less into words. It makes me know and analyze with deadly minuteness every keen, tiny damnation in my terrible lonely life. It is a mirror that shows me myself and something in myself in a merciless brilliant light, and the sight at once sickens and maddens me and fills me with an unnamed woe. It is something unspeakably dreadful. The sight for the time deadens all thought in my mind. It freezes my reason and intellect. Logic can not come to my aid. I can only feel and know the thing and it analyzes itself before my eyes.

I am alone with this—alone, alone, alone! There is no pitiful hand extended from the heights—there is no human being—ah, there is Nothing.

How can I bear it! Oh, I ask you—how can I bear it!

10 March.

MY GENIUS is an element by itself, and it is not a thing that I can tell in so many words. But it makes itself felt in every point of my life. This book would be a very different thing if I were not a genius though I am not a literary genius. Often people who come in contact with me and hear me utter a few commonplace remarks feel at once that I am extraordinary.

I am extraordinary.

I have tried longingly, passionately, to think that even this sand and barrenness is mine. But I can not. I know beyond the shadow of a doubt that it, like all good things, is beyond me. It has something that I also have. In that is our bond of sympathy.

But the sand and barrenness itself is not mine.

Always I think there is but one picture in the world more perfect in its art than the picture of me in my sand and barrenness. It is the picture of the Christ crucified with two thieves. Nothing could be more divinely appropriate. The art in it is ravishingly perfect. It is one of the few perfect pictures set before the world for all time. As I see it before my mind I can think only of its utter perfectness. I can summon no feeling of grief at the deed. The deed and the art are perfect. Its perfectness ravishes my senses.

And within me I feel that the picture of me in my sand and barrenness—knowing that even the sand and barrenness is not mine—is only second to it.

11 March.

SOMETIMES when I go out on the barrenness my mind wanders afar.

Today it went to Greece.

Oh, it was very beautiful in Greece! There was a wide, long sky that was vividly, wonderfully blue. And there was a limitless sea that was gray and green. And it went far to the south. The sky and the sea spread out into the vast world—two beautiful elements, and they fell in love with each other. And the farther away they were the nearer they moved together until at last they met and clasped each other in the far distance. There were tall, dark-green trees of kinds that are seen only in Greece. They murmured and whispered in the stillness. The wind came off from the sea and went over them and around them. They quivered and trembled in shy, ecstatic joy—for the wind was their best-beloved. There were banks of moss of a deep emerald color, and golden flowers that drooped their heavy sensual heads over to the damp black earth. And they also loved each other, and were with each other, and were glad. Clouds hung low over the sea and were dark-gray and heavy with rain. But the sun shone from behind them at intervals with beams of bronze-and-copper. Three white rocks rose up out of the sea, and the bronze-and-copper beams fell upon them, and straightway they were of gold.

Oh, how beautiful were those three gold rocks that came up out of the sea!

Aphrodite once came up out of this same sea. She came gleaming, with golden hair and beautiful eyes. Her skin glowed with tints of carmine and wild rose. Her white feet touched the smooth, yellow sand on the shore. The white feet of Aphrodite on the yellow sand made a picture of marvelous beauty. She was flushed in the joy of new life.

But the bronze-and-copper sunshine on the three white rocks was more Beautiful than Aphrodite.

I stood on the shore and looked at the rocks. My heart contracted with the pain that beautiful things bring.

The bronze-and-copper in the wide gray and green sea!

"This is the gateway of Heaven," I said to myself. "Behind those three gold rocks there is music and the high notes of happy voices." My soul grew faint. "And there is no sand and barrenness there, and no Nothingness, and no bitterness, and no hot, blinding tears. And there are no little heart-weary children, and no lonely young women—Oh, there is no loneliness at all!" My soul grew more and more faint with thinking of it. "And there is no heart there but that is pure and joyous and in Peace—in long, still, eternal Peace. And every life comes there to its own; and every earth-cry is answered, and every earth-pain is ended; and the dark spirit of Sorrow that hangs always over the earth is gone—gone,—beyond the gateway of Heaven. And more than all, Love is there and walks among the dwellers. Love is a shining figure with radiant hands, and it touches them all with its hands so that never-dying love enters into their hearts. And the love of each for another is like the love of each for self. And here at last is Truth. There is, searching and searching over the earth after Truth—and who has found it? But here is it beyond the gateway of Heaven. Those who enter in know that it is Truth at last."

And so Peace and Love and Truth are there behind the three gold rocks.

And then my soul could no longer endure the thought of it.

Suddenly the sun passed behind a heavy, dark-gray cloud, and the bronze-and-copper faded from the three rocks and left them white—very white in the wide water.

The yellow flowers laid their heads drowsily down on the emerald moss. The wind from off the sea played very gently among the motionless branches of the tall trees. The blue, blue sky and the wide, gray-green sea clasped each other more closely and mingled with each other and became one vague, shadowy element—and from it all I brought my eyes back thousands of leagues to my sand and barrenness.

The sand and barrenness is itself an element, and I have known it a long, long time.

12 March.

EVERYTHING is so dreary—so dreary.

I feel as if I would like to die to-day. I should not be the tiniest bit less unhappy afterward—but this life is unutterably weary. I am not strong. I can not bear things. I do not want to bear things. I do not long for strength. I want to be happy.

When I was very little, it was cold and dreary also, but I was certain it would be different when I should grow and be ten years old. It must be very nice to be ten, I thought,—and one would not be nearly so lonesome. But when the years passed and I was ten it was just exactly as lonesome. And when I was ten everything was very hard to understand.

But it will surely be different when I am seventeen, I said. I will know so much when I am seventeen. But when I was seventeen it was even more lonely, and everything was still harder to understand.

And again I said—faintly—everything will become clearer in a few years more, and I will wonder to think how stupid I have always been. But now the few years more have gone and here I am in loneliness that is more hopeless and harder to bear than when I was very little. Still, I wonder indeed to think how stupid I have been—and now I am not so stupid. I do not tell myself that it will be different when I am five-and-twenty.

For I know that it will not be different.

I know that it will be the same dreariness, the same

Nothingness, the same loneliness.

It is very, very lonely.

It is hope deferred and maketh the heart sick.

It is more than I can bear.

Why—*why* was I ever born!

I can not live, and I can not die—for what is there after I am dead? I can see myself wandering in dark and lonely places.

Yet I feel as if I would like to die to-day.

13 March.

IF IT were pain alone that one must bear, one could bear it. One could lose one's sense of everything but pain.

But it is pain with other things. It is the sense of pain with the sense of beauty and the sense of the anemone. And there is that mysterious pain.

Who knows the name of that mysterious pain?

It is these mingled senses that torture me.

14 March.

I HAVE been placed in this world with eyes to see and ears to hear, and I ask for Life. Is it to be wondered at? Is it so strange? Should I be content merely to see and to hear? There are other things for other people. Is it atrocious that I should ask for some other things also?

Is thy servant a dog?

15 March.

IN THESE days of approaching emotional Nature even the sand and barrenness begins to stir and rub its eyes.

My sand and barrenness is clothed in the awful majesty of countless ages. It stands always through the never-ending march of the living and the dead. It may have been green once—green and fertile, and birds and snakes and everything that loves green growing things may have lived in it. It may have sometime been rolling prairie. It may have been submerged in floods. It changed and changed in the centuries. Now it is sand and barrenness, and there are no birds and no snakes; only me. But whatever change came to it, whatever its transfiguration, the spirit of it never moved. Flood, or fertility, or rolling prairie, or barrenness—it is only itself. It has a great self, a wonderful self.

I shall never forget you, my sand and barrenness.

Some day, shall my thirsty life be watered, my starved heart fed, my asking voice answered, my tired soul taken into the warmth of another with the intoxicating sweetness of love?

It may be.

But I shall remember the sand and barrenness that is with me in my Nothingness. The sand and barrenness and the memory of the anemone lady are all that are in any degree mine.

And so then I shall remember it.

As I stand among the barren gulches in these days and look away at the slow-awakening hills of Montana, I hear the high, swelling, half-tired, half-hopeful song of the world. As I listen I know that there are things, other than the Virtue and the Truth and the Love, that are not for me. There is beyond me, like these, the unbreaking, undying bond of human fellowship—a thing that is earth-old.

It is beyond me, and it is nothing to me.

In my intensest desires—in my widest longings—I never go beyond *self*. The ego is the all.

Limitless legions of women and men in weariness and in joy are one. They are killing each other and torturing each other, and going down in sorrow to the dust. But they are one. Their right hands are joined in unseen sympathy and kinship.

But my two hands are apart, and clasped together in an agony of loneliness.

I have read of women who have been strongly, grandly brave. Sometimes I have dreamed that I might be brave. The possibilities of this life are magnificent.

To be saturated with this agony, I say at times, and to bear with it all; not to sink beneath it, but to vanquish it, and to make it the grace and comeliness of my entire life from the Beginning to the End!

Perhaps a woman—a real woman—could do this.

But I?—No. I am not real—I do not seem *real* to myself. In such things as these my life is a blank.

There was Charlotte Corday—a heroine whom I admire above all the heroines. And more than she was a heroine she was a woman. And she had her agony. It was for love of her fair country.

To suffer and do and die for love of something! It is glorious! What must be the exalted ecstasy of Charlotte Corday's soul now!

And I—with all my manifold passions—I am a coward.

I have had moments when, vaguely and from far off, it seemed as if there might be bravery and exaltation for me,—when I could rise far over myself. I have felt unspeakable possibilities. While they lasted—what wonderful emotion was it that I felt?

But they are not real.

They fade away—they fade away.

And again come the varied phenomena of my life to bewilder and terrify me.

Confusion! Chaos! Damnation! They are not moments of exaltation now. Poor little Mary MacLane!

"If to do were as easy as to know what were good to do, chapels had been churches, and poor men's cottages princes' palaces."

I do not know what to do.

I do not know what were good to do.

I would do nothing if I knew.

I might add to my litany this: Most kind Devil, deliver me—from myself.

16 MARCH.

TODAY I walked over the sand, and it was almost beautiful. The sun was sinking and the sky was filled with roses and gold.

Then came my soul and confronted me. My soul is wondrous fair. It is like a young woman. The beauty of it is too great for human eyes to look upon. It is too great for mine. Yet I look.

My soul said to me: "I am sick."

I answered: "And I am sick."

"We may be well," said my soul. "Why are we not well?"

"How may we be well?" I asked.

"We may throw away all our vanity and false pride," said my soul. "We may take on a new life. We may learn to wait and to possess ourselves in patience. We may labor and overcome."

"We can do none of these things," I cried. "Have I not tried all of them some time in my short life? And have I not waited and wanted until you have become faint with pain? Have I not looked and longed? Dear soul, why do you not resign yourself? Why can you not stay quiet and trouble yourself and me no more? Why are you always straining and reaching? There isn't anything for you. You are wearing yourself out."

My soul made answer: "I may strain and reach until only one worn nerve of me is left. And that one nerve may be scourged with whips and burned with fire. But I will keep one atom of faith. I may go bad, but I will keep one atom of faith in Love and in the Truth that is Love. You are a genius, but I am no genius. The years—a million of years—may do their utmost to destroy the single nerve. They may lash and beat it. I will keep my one atom of faith.

"You are not wise," I said. "You have been wandering and longing for a time that seems a thousand years—through my cold, dark childhood to my cold, dark womanhood. Is that not enough to quiet you? Is that not enough to teach you the lesson of Nothing? You are not a genius, but you are not a fool."

"I will keep my one atom of faith," said my soul.

"But lie and sleep now," I said. "Don't reach after that Light any more. Let us both sleep a few years."

"No," said my soul.

"Oh, my soul" I wailed, "look away at that glowing copper horizon—and beyond it. Let us go there now and take an infinite rest. Now! We can bear this no longer."

"No," said my soul; "we will stay here and bear more. There would be no rest yet beyond the copper horizon. And there is no need of going anywhere. I have my one atom of faith."

I gazed at my soul as it stood plainly before me, weak and worn and faint, in the fading light. It had one atom of faith, it said, and tried to hold its head high and to look strong and triumphant. Oh, the irony—the pathos of it!

My soul, with its one pitiful atom of faith, looked only what it was—a weeping, hunted thing.

17 MARCH.

IN SOME rare between-whiles it is as if nothing mattered. My heart aches, I say; my soul wanders; this person or that person was repelled today; but nothing matters.

A great inner languor comes like a giant and lays hold of me. I lie fallow beneath it.

Some one forgot me in the giving of things. But it does not matter. I feel nothing.

Persons say to me, don't analyze any more and you will not be unhappy.

When Something throws heavy clubs at you and you are hit by them, don't be hurt. When Something stronger than you holds your hands in the fire, don't let it burn you. When Something pushes you into a river of ice, don't be cold. When something draws a cutting lash across your naked shoulders, don't let it concern you—don't be conscious that it is there.

This is great wisdom and fine, clear logic.

It is a pity that no one has ever yet been able to live by it.

But after all it's no matter. Nothing is any one's affair. It is all of no consequence.

And have I not had all my anguish for nothing? I am a fool—a fool.

A handful of rich black mud in a pig's yard—does it wonder why it is there? Does it torture itself about the other mud around it, and about the earth and water of which it is made, and about the pig? Only fool's mud would do so. And so, then, I am fool's mud.

Nothing counts. Nothing can possibly count.

Regret, passion, cowardice, hope, bravery, unrest, pain, the love-sense, the soul-sense, the beauty-sense—all for nothing! What can a handful of rich black mud in a pig's yard have to do with these? I am a handful of rich black mud—a fool-woman, fool's mud.

All on earth that I need to do is to lie still in the hot sun and feel the pig rolling and floundering and slushing about. It were folly to waste my mud nerves in wondering. Be quiet, fool-woman, let things be. Your soul is a fool's-mud soul and is governed by the pig; your heart is a fool's-mud heart, and wants nothing beyond the pig; your life is a fool's-mud life, and is the pig's life.

Something within me shrieks now, but I do not know what it is—nor why it shrieks.

It groans and moans.

There is no satisfaction in being a fool—no satisfaction at all.

18 MARCH.

BUT yes. It all matters, whether or no. Nature is one long battle, and the never-ending perishing of the weak. I must grind and grind away. I have no choice. And I must know that I grind.

Fool, genius, young lonely woman—I must go round and round in the life within, for how many years the Devil knows. After that my soul must go round and round, for how many centuries the Devil knows.

What a master-mind is that of the Devil! The world is a wondrous scheme. For me it is a scheme that is black with woe. But there may be in the world some one who finds it beautiful Real Life.

I wonder as I write this Portrayal if there will be one person to read it and see a thing that is mingled with every word. It is something that you must feel, that must fascinate you, the like of which you have never before met with.

It is the unparalleled individuality of me.

I wish I might write it in so many words of English. But that is not possible. If I have put it in every word and if you feel it and are fascinated, then I have done very well.

I am marvelously clever if I have done so.

I know that I am marvelously clever. But I have need of all my peculiar genius to show you my individuality—my aloneness.

I am alone out on my sand and barrenness. I should be alone if my sand and barrenness were crowded with a thousand people each filled with melting sympathy for me—though it would be unspeakably sweet.

People say of me, "She's peculiar." They do not understand me. If they did they would say so oftener and with emphasis.

And so I try to put my individuality in the quality of my diction, in my method of handling words.

My conversation plainly shows this individuality—more than shows it, indeed. My conversation hurls it violently at people's heads. My conversation—when I choose—makes people turn around in their chairs and stare and give me all of their attention. They admire me, though their admiration is mixed decidedly with other feelings.

I like to be admired.

It soothes my vanity.

When you read this Portrayal you will admire me. You will surely have to admire me.

And so this is life, and everything matters.

But just now I will stop writing and go downstairs to my dinner. There is a porterhouse steak, broiled rare, and some green young onions. Oh, they are good! And when one is to have a porterhouse steak for one's dinner—and some green young onions, one doesn't give a tupenny damn whether anything else matters or not.

19 MARCH.

ON A day when the sky is like lead and a dull, tempestuous wilderness of gray clouds adds a dreariness to the sand, there is added to the loneliness of my life a deep bitterness of gall and wormwood.

Out of my bitterness it is easy for bad to come.

Surely Badness is a deep black pool wherein one may

drown dullness and Nothingness.

I do not know Badness well. It is something material that seems a great way off now, but that might creep nearer and nearer as I became less and less young.

But now when the day is of the leaden dullness I look at Badness and long for it. I am young and all alone, and everything that is good is beyond my reach. But all that is bad—surely that is within the reach of every one.

I wish for a long pageant of bad things to come and whirl and rage through this strange leaden life of mine and break the spell.

Why should it not be Badness instead of Death? Death, it seems, will bring me but a change of agony. Badness would perhaps so crowd my life with its vivid phenomena that they would act as a neurotic to the racked nerves of my Nothingness. It would be an outlet—and possibly I could forget some things.

I think just now of a woman who lived long ago and in whom the world at large seems not to have found anything admirable. I mean Messalina Valeria, the wife of the stupid emperor Claudius. I have conceived a profound admiration for this historic wanton. She may not indeed have had anything to forget; she may not have suffered. But she had the strength of will to take what she wanted, to do as she liked, to live as she chose to live.

It is admirable and beautiful beyond expression to sacrifice and give up and wait for love of that good that gives in itself a just reward. And only next to this is the throwing to the winds of all restraint when the good holds itself aloof and gives nothing. We are weak, contemptible fools who do not grasp the resources within our reach when there is no just reward for our restraint. Why do we not take what we want of the various temptations? It is not that we are virtuous. It is that we are cowards.

And it is worth while to remain true to an ideal that offers only the vaguest hopes of realization? It is not philosophy. When one has made up one's mind that one wants a dish of hot stewed mushrooms, and set one's heart on it, should one scorn a handful of raw evaporated apples, if one were starving, for the sake of the phantom dish of hot stewed mushrooms? Should one say, Let me starve, but I will never descend to evaporated apples; I will have nothing but a dish of hot stewed mushrooms?

If one is sure one will have the stewed mushrooms finally, before one dies of starvation, then very well. One should wait for them and take nothing else.

But it is not in my good peripatetic philosophy to pass by the Badness that the gods provide for the sake of a faraway, always-unrealized ideal, however brilliant, however beautiful, however golden.

When the lead is in the sky and in my life, a vision of Badness looms up on the horizon and looks at me and beckons with a fascinating finger. Then I say to myself, What is the use of this unsullied, struggling soul; this unbesmirched, empty heart; this treasureless, innocent mind; this insipid maid's-body? There are no good things for them. But here, to be sure, are fascinating, glittering bad things—the goods that the gods provide, the compensation of the Devil.

Comes Death, some day, I said—but to die, in the sight of glittering bad things—and I only nineteen! These glittering things appear fair.

There is really nothing evil in the world. Some things appear distorted and unnatural because they have been badly done. Had they been perfect in conception and execution they would strike one only with admiration at their fine, iridescent lights. You remember Don Juan and Haidee. That, to be sure, was not evil in any event—they loved each other. But if they had had only a passing, if intense, fancy for one another, who would call it evil? Who would call it anything but wonderful, charming, enchanting? The Devil's bad things—like the Devil's good things—may gleam and glisten, oh, how they may gleam and glisten! I have seen them do so, not only in a poem of Byron's, but in the life that is.

Always when the lead is in the sky I would like to cultivate thoroughly this branch of the vineyard. Now doesn't it make you shiver to think of this dear little Mary MacLane wandering unloved through dark by-ways and deadly labyrinths? It makes me shiver. But it needn't. If I am to wander unloved, why not as well wander there as through Nothingness?

I fancy it must be wonderfully easy to become used to the many-sided Badness. I have lived my nineteen years in the midst of Nothingness, and I have not yet become used to it. It has sharp knives in it, has Nothingness. Badness may have some sharp knives also—but there are other things. Yes, there are other things.

Kind Devil, if you are not to fetch me Happiness, then slip off from your great steel key-ring a bright little key to the door of the glittering, gleaming bad things, and give it me, and show me the way, and wish me joy.

I would like to live about seven years of judicious Badness, and then Death, if you will. Nineteen years of damnable Nothingness, seven years of judicious Badness—and then Death. A noble ambition! But might it not be worse? If not that, then nineteen years of damnable Nothingness, and then Death. No; when the lead is in the sky that does not appeal to me. My versatile mind turns to the seven years of judicious Badness.

There is nothing in the world without its element of Badness. It is in literature; it is in every art—in pictures, sculpture, even in music. There are certain fine, deep, minute passages in Beethoven and in Chopin that tell of things wonderfully, sublimely bad. Chopin one can not understand. Is there any one in the world who can understand him? But we know at once that there is the Badness—and it is music!

There is the element of Badness in me.

I long to cultivate my element of Badness. Badness compared to Nothingness is beautiful. And so, then, I wait also for some one to come over the hill with things other than Happiness. But whatever I wait for, nothing comes.

20 MARCH.

THERE were pictures in the red sunset sky today. I looked at them and was racked with passions of desire. I fancied to myself that I could have any of the good things in the pictures for the asking and the waiting. The while I knew that when the sunset should fade from the sky I would be overwhelmed by my heaviest woe.

There was a picture of intense peace. There were stretches of flat, green country, and oak-trees and aspens, and a still, still lake. In the dim distance you could see fields of wheat and timothy-grass that moved a little as if in the wind. You could fancy the cows feeding just below the brow of the near hills, and a hawk floating and wheeling among the clouds. A rainbow arched over the lake. There is nothing lacking here, I thought. "Life and health and peace possessing." Give me this, kind Devil.

There was a picture of endless, limitless strength. There were the oak-trees again but bereft now of every leaf, and the bristling, jagged rocks back of them were not more coldly staunch. The sun poured brilliantly bright upon them. A river flowed unmoved and quiet between yellow clay banks. A tornado might sweep over this and not one twig would be displaced, not one ripple would come to the river. Is it not fine! I said to myself. No feeling, no self-analysis, no aching, no pain—and the strength of the Philistines. Oh, kind Devil, I entreat you, let me have that!

There was a picture of untrammeled revel and forgetfulness. There were fields of swaying daffodils and red lilies. The young shrubs tossed their heads and were joyous. Lambs gamboled and the happy meadow-lark knew whereof she sang.

The winds with wonder whist
Smoothly the waters kissed.

Be carefree, be light-hearted, be wicked—above all, forget. The deeds are what you will; the time is now; the aftermath is nothing; the day of reckoning is never. Love things lightly, take all that you see, and to the winds with regret! Gracious Devil, I whispered intensely, give me this and no other!

There was a picture of raging elements. "The winds blew, and the rains descended and the floods came." The sky was overcast with rolling clouds. The air was heavy with unrest. There was a gray stone house set upon a rocky point, and I had momentary glimpses of an unquiet sea below it. Back on the surface of the land slender trees were waving wildly in the gale. The wind and the rain were saying, "Damn you, little earth, I have you now,—I will rend and ruin you." They whipped and raged in frenzied joy. The little earth liked it. The elements whirled and whistled round the gray stone house. A lurid light came from a ghastly moon between clouds. The entire scene was desolately savage and forlorn, but attractive. As I listened in fancy to that shrieking, wailing wind, and saw green branches jerked and twisted asunder in the storm, my barren, defrauded heart leaped and exulted. If I could live in the midst of this and be beaten and shaken roughly, would not that deep sense forget to ache? Kind Devil, pray send me some storms. It is Nothingness that bears down heavy.

There was a picture of an exalted spiritual life. There was that strange bright light. And the things in the picture were those things alone in this world that are real, and the only things that count. The old, soft green of the old, old rolling hills was the green of love—the earth-love and the love that comes from beyond the earth. The air and the blue water and the sunshine were so beautifully real and true that except for their deep-reaching, passionate tenderness human strength could not endure them. There were lanes of climbing vines and white violets. Was it my fancy that brought their thin fragrance to me over piles of billowy clouds? There was something there that was old—old as the race. Those green valleys were the same as when the mists first lifted from the earth. As I looked my life stood still. My soul shivered faintly. As I looked I felt nearer, my God, to thee—though I have no God and everything is away from me, nothing tender comes to me.

Still it was nearer, my God, to thee.

A voice came out of the far, far distant ages and said very gently: "All these shadows are falling in vain. You are blinded and bewildered in the darkness—the darkness is deep—deep. There is not one dim ray of light. Your feet falter and stumble. You can not see. But the shadows are falling in vain."

I ask you, Why is this life not mine?

I implore and wring my hands in agonized entreaty, and almost it seems sometimes my fingers can grasp these things—but there is something cold and strong between them and me. Oh, what is it!

There was a picture of various castles in Spain. They were most beautiful, were those castles. The lights that shone on the battlements were soft, bright lights. For one thing, I fancied I saw myself and Fame with me. Fame is very fine. The sun and moon and stars may go dark in the Heavens. Bitter rain may fall out of the clouds. But never mind. Fame has a sun and moon and gently brilliant stars of her own, and these, shining once, shine always. The green river may run dry in the land. But Fame has a green river that never runs dry. One may wander over the face of the earth. But Fame is herself a refuge. One may be a target for stones and mud. Yes—but Fame stands near with her arm laid across one's shoulders—as no other arm can be laid across one's shoulders. Fame would fill several empty places. Fame would continue to fill them for some years.

Fame, if you please, Devil.

There was a picture of Death. I saw a figure lying in the midst of a desert that was rather like my sand and barrenness. Not far off a wolf sat on his haunches and waited for the end. A buzzard perched near and waited also. They both appeared hungry. It seemed as though the end might come quickly.

Let it come, kind Devil.

And a wolf and a buzzard are better than an undertaker and some worms. Although that doesn't much matter.

And oh, there again was the dearest picture of all—the red, red picture of Happiness for me, Happiness with the sunshine falling on the Heaven-kissing hills! There was I, and I loved and was loved. I—out of loneliness into perfect Happiness! The yellow-gold of the glorious hot sun melted and poured over the earth and over everything that was there. The river ran and rippled and sang the most sweetly glad song that ever river sang. Winged things sparkled in the gold light and flew down the sky. "The wonderful air was over me; the wonderful wind was shaking the tree." The silent voices in the air rang out like flutes and clarionets. And the love of the man-devil for me was everywhere—above me, around me, within me. It would last for a number of beautiful yellow-gold days. I—out of the anguish of loneliness into this!

My heart is filled with desire.

My soul is filled with passion.

My life is a life of longing.

All pictures fade before this picture. They fade completely. When the sun itself faded I gazed over my sand and barrenness with blurred, unseeing eyes and wished only with a heavy, desolate spirit for the coming of the Devil.

21 March.

SOME people think, absurdly enough, that to be Scotch or descended from the Scottish clans is to be rather strong, rather conservative, firm in faith, and all that. The idea is one that should be completely exploded by this time. I think that the Scotch as a nation are the most difficult of all to characterize. Their traits and tendencies cover a wider field than those of any other. To be Scotch is to be anything. There is no man so narrow as a Scotchman. There is no man so broad as a Scotchman. There is no mind so versatile as a Scotch mind. At the same time only a Scotch mind is capable of clinging with bull-dog tenacity to one idea. A Scotch heart out of all, and through all, can be true as death. A Scotch heart—the same one—can be cunning and treacherous as false human hearts are made. To be English is to have limits; the Germans, the French, the Russians—they have all some inevitable attributes to modify their genius.

But one may be anything—anything, if one is Scotch.

Always I think of the cruel, hardened, ferocious, weather-beaten, kilted Clan MacLean wandering over bleak winter hills, fighting the powerful MacDonalds and MacGregors—and generally wiping them from the earth,—marching away with merrily shrieking pipes from fields of withered, blood-soaked heather—and all this merely to gather intensified life for me. I feel that the causes of my tragedy began long, long ago from remote germs.

My Scotch blood added to my genius sense has made me into a dangerous chemical compound. By analyzing I have brought an almost clear portrait of myself up before my mind's eyes.

When I was a child I did not analyze knowingly, but the child was this same genius, though I am one of the kind that changes widely and decidedly in the years. This weary unhappiness is not a matter of development.

When I was a child I felt dumbly what I feel now less dumbly. At the age of five I used sometimes to weep silently in the night—I did not know why. It was that I felt my aloneness, my foreignness to all things. I felt the heavy, heavy weight of life—and I was only five.

I was only five, and it seems a thousand years ago. But sometimes back through the long, winding, unused passages of my mind I hear that silent sobbing of the child and the unarmed wailing of a tiny, tired soul.

It mingles with the bitter Nothingness of the grown young woman, and oh, with it all—with it all I am so unhappy!

There is something subtly *Scotch* in all this.

But Scotch or Indian or Japanese, there is no stopping of the pain.

22 MARCH.

I FEAR, do you know, fine world, that you do not yet know me really well—particularly me of the flesh. Me of the peculiar philosophy and the unhappy spirit you know rather well by now, unless you are stupider than I think you are. But you might pass me in the street—you might spend the day with me—and never suspect that I am I. Though for the matter of that, even if I had set before you a most graphic and minutely drawn portrait of myself, I am certainly clever enough to act a quite different role if I chose—when you came to spend the day. Still, if the world at large is to know me as I desire it to know me without ever seeing me, I shall have to bring myself into closer personal range with it—and you may rise in your seats and focus your opera-glasses, stare with open mouths, stand on your hind-legs and gape—I will myself turn on glaring green and orange lights from the wings.

I believe that it's the trivial little facts about anything that describe it the most effectively. In *Vanity Fair*, when Becky Sharpe was describing young Crawley in a letter to her friend Amelia, she stated that he had hay-colored whiskers and straw-colored hair. And knowing this you feel that you know much more about the Crawley than you would if Miss Sharpe had not mentioned those things. And yet it is but a mere matter of color!

When you think that Dickens was extremely fond of cats you feel at once that nothing could be more fitting. Somehow that marvelously mingled humor and pathos and gentle irony seem to go exceedingly well with a fondness for soft, green-eyed, purring things. If you had not read the pathetic humor, but knew about Dickens and his warm feline friends you might easily expect such things from him.

When you read somewhere that Dr. Johnson is said never to have washed his neck and his ears, and then go and read some of his powerful, original philosophy, you say to yourself, "Yes, I can readily believe that this man never troubled himself to wash his neck and his ears." I, for my part, having read some of the things he has written, can not reconcile myself to the fact that he ever washed any part of his anatomy. I admire Dr. Johnson—though I wash my own neck occasionally.

When you think of Napoleon amusing himself by taking a child on his knee and pinching it to hear it cry, you feel an ecstatic little wave of pleasure at the perfect fitness of things. You think of his hard, brilliant, continuous victories, and you suspect that Napoleon Bonaparte lived but to gratify Napoleon Bonaparte. When you think of the heavy, muscular man smilingly pinching the child, you are quite sure of it. Such a method of amusement for that king among men is so exquisitely appropriate that you wonder why you had not thought of it yourself.

So, then, yes. I believe strenuously in the efficacy of seemingly trivial facts as portrayers of one's character—one's individual humanness.

Now I will set down for your benefit divers and varied observations relative to me—an interesting one of womankind and nineteen years, and curious and fascinating withal.

Well, then.

Nearly every day I make me a plate of hot, rich fudge, with brown sugar (I should be an entirely different person if I made it with white sugar—and the fudge would not be nearly so good), and take it upstairs to my room, with a book or a newspaper. My mind then takes in a part of what is contained in the book or the newspaper, and the stomach of the MacLane takes in all of what is contained in the plate. I sit by my window in a miserable, uncomfortable, stiff-backed chair, but I relieve the strain by resting my feet on the edge of the low bureau. Usually the book that I read is an old dilapidated bound volume of that erstwhile periodical, "Our Young Folks." It is a thing that possesses a charm for me. I never grow tired of it. As I eat my nice brown little squares of fudge I read about a boy whose name is Jack Hazard and who, J. T. Trowbridge informs the reader, is doing his best, and who seems to find it somewhat difficult. I believe I could repeat pages of J. T. Trowbridge from memory, and that ancient bound volume has become a part of my life. I stop reading after a few minutes, but I continue to eat—and gaze at the toes of my shoes which need polishing badly, or at the conglomeration of brilliant pictures on my bedroom wall, or out of the window at the children playing in the street. But mostly I gaze without seeing, and my versatile mind is engaged either in nothing or in repeating something over and over, such as, "But the sweet face of Lucy Gray will never more be seen." Only I am not aware that I have been repeating it until I happen to remember it afterward.

Always the fudge is very good, and I eat and eat with unabated relish until all the little squares are gone. A very little of my fudge has been known to give some people a most terrific stomach-ache—but my own digestive organs seem to like nothing better. It's so brown—so rich!

I amuse myself with this for an hour or two in the afternoon. Then I go downstairs and work awhile.

There are few things that annoy me so much as to be called a young lady. I am no lady—as any one could see by close inspection, and the phrase has an odious sound. I would rather be called a sweet little thing, or a fallen woman, or a sensible girl—though they would each be equally a lie.

Always I am glad when night comes and I can sleep. My mind works busily repeating things while I divest myself of my various dusty garments. As I remove a dozen or two of hairpins from my head I say within me:

You are old, father William, one would hardly suppose
That your eye is as steady as ever;
Yet you balanced an eel on the end of your nose—
What made you so awfully clever?

Always I take a little clock to bed with me and hang it by a cord at the head of my bed for company. I have named the clock Little Fido, because it is so constant and ticks always. It is beginning to stand in the same relation to me as J. T.

Trowbridge's magazine. If I were to go away from here I should take Little Fido and the magazine with me.

Every morning, being beautifully hungry after my walk, I eat three boiled eggs out of the shell for my breakfast. The while I mentally thank the kind Providence that invented hens. Also I eat bits of toast. I have my breakfast alone—because the rest of the family are still sleeping,—sitting at a corner of the kitchen table. I enjoy those three eggs and those bits of toast. Usually when I am eating my breakfast I am thinking of three things: the varying price of any eggs that are fit to eat; of what to do after I've finished my housework and before lunch; and of my one friend. And I meditatively and gently kick the leg of the table with the heel of my right foot.

I have beautiful hair.

In the front of my shirt-waist there are nine cambric handkerchiefs cunningly distributed. My figure is very pretty, to be sure, but not so well developed as it will be in five years—if I live so long. And so I help it out materially with nine cambric handkerchiefs. You can see by my picture that my waist curves gracefully out. Only it is not all flesh—some of it is handkerchief. It amuses me to do this. It is one of my petty vanities.

Likewise by an ingenious arrangement of my striped moreen petticoat I contrive to display a more evident pair of hips than Nature seems to have intended for me at this stage. Doubtless they also will take on fuller proportions when some years have passed. Still I am not dissatisfied with them as they are. It is not as if they were too well developed—in which case I should have need of all my skill in arranging my moreen petticoat so as to lessen their effect. It is easy enough to add on to these things, but one would experience serious difficulty in attempting to take from them. I hate that heavy, aggressive kind of hips. Moreover, small, graceful ones are desirable when one is nineteen. The world at large judges you more leniently on that account—usually. Narrow, shapely hips may give one an effect of youth and harmlessness which is a distinct advantage, when, for instance, one is writing a Portrayal and so will be at the world's mercy. I believe I should not think of attempting to write a Portrayal if I had hips like a pair of saddle-bags. Certainly it would avail me nothing.

Sometimes I look at my face in a mirror and find it not plain but ugly. And there are other times when I look and find it not pretty but beautiful with a Madonna-like sweetness.

I told you I might say more about the liver that is within me before I have done. Well, then, I will say this: that the world, if it had a liver like mine, would be very different from what it is. The world would be many-colored and mobile and passionate and nervous and high-strung and intensely alive and poetic and romantic and philosophical and egotistic and pathetic, and, oh, racked to the verge of madness with the spirit of unrest—if the world had a liver like mine. It is not all of these now. It is rather stupid. Gods and little fishes! would not the world be wonderful if all in it were like me? And it would be if it had a liver like mine. For it is my liver mostly that makes me what I am—apart from my genius. My liver is fine and perfect, but sensitive, and, well—it's a dangerous thing to have within you.

It is the liver of the MacLanes.

It is the foundation of the curious castle of my existence.

And after all, fine, brave, stupid world, you may be grateful to the Devil that yours is not like it.

I have seventeen little engraved portraits of Napoleon that I keep in one of my bureau-drawers. Often late in the evening, between nine and ten o'clock, when I come in from a walk over the sand and barrenness, I take these pictures from the drawer and gaze at them carefully a long time and think of that man until I am stirred to the depths.

And then easily and naturally I fall in love with Napoleon.

If only he were living now, I think to myself, I would make my way to him by whatever means and cast myself at his feet. I would entreat him with the most passionate humbleness of spirit to take me into his life for three days. To be the wife of Napoleon for three days—that would be enough for a lifetime! I would be much more than satisfied if I could get three such days out of life.

I suppose a man is either a villain or a fool, though some of them seem to be a judicious mingling of both. The type of the distinct villain is preferable to a mixture of the two, and to a plain fool. I like a villain anyway—a villain that can be rather tender at times. And so, then, as I look at the pictures I fall in love with the incomparable Napoleon. The seventeen pictures are all different and all alike. I fall in love with each picture separately.

In one he is ugly and unattractive—and strong. I fall in love with him.

In another he is cruel and heartless and utterly selfish—and strong. I fall in love with him.

In a third he has a fat, pudgy look, and is quite insignificant—and strong. I fall in love with him.

In a fourth he is grandly sad and full of despair—and strong. I fall in love with him.

In the fifth he is greasy and greedy and common-looking—and strong. I fall in love with him.

In the sixth he is masterly and superior and exalted—and strong. I fall in love with him.

In the seventh he is romantic and beautiful—and strong. I fall in love with him.

In the eighth he is obviously sensual and reeking with uncleanness—and strong. I fall in love with him.

In the ninth he is unearthly and mysterious and unreal—and strong. I fall in love with him.

In the tenth he is black and sullen-browed, and ill-humored—and strong. I fall in love with him.

In the eleventh he is inferior and trifling and inane—and strong. I fall in love with him.

In the twelfth he is rough and ruffianly and uncouth—and strong. I fall in love with him.

In the thirteenth he is little and wolfish and vile—and strong. I fall in love with him.

In the fourteenth he is calm and confident and intellectual—and strong. I fall in love with him.

In the fifteenth he is vacillating and fretful and his mouth is like a woman's—and still he is strong. I fall in love with him.

In the sixteenth he is slow and heavy and brutal—and strong. I fall in love with him.

In the seventeenth he is rather tender—and strong. I fall vividly in love with him.

Napoleon was rather like the Devil, I think as I sit in the straight-backed chair with my feet on the bureau and gaze long and intently at the seventeen pictures, late in the evening.

Then I wearily put them away, maddened with the sense of Nothingness, and take Little Fido and go to bed.

Sometimes, early in the evening just before dinner, I sit in the stiff-backed chair with my elbows on the window-sill and my head resting on one hand, and I look out of the window at a Pile of Stones and a Barrel of Lime. These are in the vacant lot next to this house.

I fix my eyes intently on the Pile of Stones and the Barrel of Lime. And I fix my thoughts on them also. And some of my widest thoughts come to me then.

I feel an overwhelming wave of a kind of pantheism which, at the moment I feel it, begins slowly to grow less and less and continues in this until finally it dwindles to a Pile of Stones and a Barrel of Lime.

I feel at the moment that the universe is a Pile of Stones and a Barrel of Lime. They alone are the Real Things.

Take anything at any point and deceive yourself into thinking that you are happy with it. But look at it heavily; dig down underneath the layers and layers of rose-colored mists and you will find that your Thing is a Pile of Stones and a Barrel of Lime.

A struggle or two, a fight, an agony, a passing—and then the only Real Things: a Pile of Stones and a Barrel of Lime.

Damn everything! Afterward you will find that you have done all your damning for naught. For there is nothing worthy of damnation except a Pile of Stones and a Barrel of Lime—and they are not damnable. They have never harmed you, and moreover they alone are the Real Things.

Julius Caesar made many wars. Sir Francis Drake went sailing over the seas. It was all child's play and counts for nothing. Here are the Pile of Stones and a Barrel of Lime.

And so this is how it is early in the evening just before dinner, when I sit in the uncomfortable chair with my elbows on the window-sill and my head resting on one hand.

I have two pictures of Marie Bashkirtseff high upon my wall. Often I lean my head on the back of the chair with my feet on the bureau—always with my feet on the bureau—and look at these pictures.

In one of them she is eighteen years old and wears a green

frock which is extremely becoming—of which fact the person inside of it seems fully aware. The other picture is taken from her last photograph, when she was twenty-four.

Marie Bashkirtseff is a very beautiful creature. And evidently *she* is not obliged to arrange a moreen petticoat over her plumpness. She has a wonderfully voluptuous look for a woman of eighteen years. In the later picture vanity is written in every line of her graceful form and in every feature of that charming face. The picture fairly yells: "I am Marie Bashkirtseff—and, oh, I am splendid!"

And as I look at the pictures I am glad. For though she was admirable and splendid, and all, she was no such genius as I. She had a genius of her own, it is true. But the Bashkirtseff, with her voluptuous body and her attractive personality, is after all a bit ordinary. My genius, though not powerful, is rare and deep, and no one has ever had or ever will have a genius like it.

Mary MacLane, if you live—if you live, my darling, the world will one day recognize your genius. And when once the world has recognized such genius as this—oh, then no one will ever think of profaning it by comparing it with any Bashkirtseff!

But I would give up this genius eagerly, gladly—at once and forever—for one dear, bright day free from loneliness.

The portraits of the Bashkirtseff are certainly beautiful, but there is something about them that is—well, not common, but bourgeois at least, as if she were a German waitress of unusual appearance, or an aristocratic shop-girl, or a nurse with good taste who would walk out on pleasant forenoons wheeling a go-cart—something of that sort. Perhaps it is because her neck is too short, or because her wrists are too muscular-looking. I thank a gracious Devil as I look up at the pictures that I have not those particular points and that particular bourgeois air. I am bound to confess that I have one of my own, but mine is Highland Scotch—and anyway, I am Mary MacLane.

Marie Bashkirtseff is beautiful enough, however, that she can easily afford to look rather second-rate.

I like to look at my two pictures of her.

I value money literally for its own sake. I like the feeling of dollars and quarters rubbing softly together in my hand. Always it reminds me of those lovely chestfuls of gold that Captain Kidd buried—no one seems to know just where. Usually I keep some fairly-clean dollars and quarters to handle. "Money is so nice!" I say to myself.

If you think, fine world, that I am always interesting and striking and admirable, always original, showing up to good advantage in a company of persons, and all—why, then you are beautifully mistaken. There are times, to be sure, when I can rivet the attention of the crowd heavily upon myself. But mostly I am the very least among all the idiots and fools. I show up to the poorest possible advantage.

Of several ways that are mine there is one that gives me a distinct and hopeless air of insignificance. I have seen people, having met me for the first time, glance carelessly at me as if they were quite sure I had not an idea in my brain—if I had a brain; as if they wondered why I had been asked there; as if they were fully aware that they had but to fiddle and "It" would dance. Sometimes before this highly intellectual gathering breaks up I manage to make them change their minds with astonishing suddenness. But nearly always I don't bother about it at all. I go among people occasionally because it amuses me. It may be a literary club where they talk theosophy, or it may be a Cornish dance where they have pasty and saffron cake and the chief amusement is sending beer-bottles at various heads, or it may be a lady-like circle of married women with cerise silk drop-skirts and white kid gloves, drinking chocolate in the afternoon and talking about something "shocking!"

And often, as I say, I am the least of them.

Genius is an odd thing.

When certain of my skirts need sewing, they don't get sewed. I simply pin the rents in them together and it lasts as long or longer than if I had seated myself in my stiff-backed chair with a needle and thread and mended them—like a sensible girl. (I hate a sensible girl.)

Though I have never yet hurriedly pinned up a torn flounce or several inches of skirt-binding without saying softly to myself, using a trite, expressive phrase, "Certainly, it's a hell of a way to do." Still I never take a needle and mend my garments. I couldn't, anyway. I never learned to sew, and I don't intend ever to learn. It reminds me too much of a constipated dressmaker.

And so I pin up the torn places—though, as I say, I never fail to make use of the quaint, expressive phrase.

All of which a reasonably astute reader will recognize as an important point in the portraying of any character—whether mine or the queen of Spain's.

I had for my dinner to-day some whole-wheat bread, some liver-and-bacon, and some green, green early asparagus. While I was eating these the world seemed a very nice place indeed.

I never see people walking along on the opposite side of the street, as I sit by my window, without wondering who they are, and how they live, and how ugly they would look if their bodies were not adorned with clothes. Always I feel certain that some of them are bow-legged.

And sometimes I see a woman in a fearful state of deshabille walk across the vacant lot next to this. "A plague on me," I say then to myself, "if I ever become middle-aged and if my entire being seems to tip up in the front, and if I go about with no stays so that when I tie an apron around my waist my upper fatness hangs over the band like a natural blouse."

And so—I could go on writing all night these seemingly trivial but really significant details relating to the outer genius. But these will answer. These to any one who knows things will be a revelation.

Sometimes you know things, fine brave world.

You must know likewise that though I do ordinary things, when *I* do them they cease to be ordinary. I make fudge—and a sweet girl makes fudge, but there are ways and ways of doing things. This entire affair of the fudge is one of my uniquest points.

No sweet girl makes fudge and eats it, as I make fudge and eat it.

So it is.

But, oh—who is to understand all this? Who will understand any of this Portrayal? My unhappy soul has delved in shadows far, far beyond and below.

23 MARCH.

MY PHILOSOPHY, I find after very little analysis, approaches precariously near to sensualism.

It is wonderful how many sides there can be to just one character.

Nature, with all those suns, and all those hilltops, and all those rivers, and all those stars, is inscrutable—intangible—maddening. It affects one with unutterable joy and anguish, but no one can ever begin to understand what it means.

Human nature is yet more inscrutable—and nothing appears on the surface. One can have no idea of the things buried in the minds of one's acquaintances. And mostly they are fools and have no idea themselves of what germs are in themselves—of what they are capable. And in most minds it is true the dormant devils never awaken and never are known.

It is another sign of my analytical genius, that I, aged nineteen, recognize the devils in my character. I have not the slightest wish, since things are as they are with me, to rid myself of them. There is in me much more of evil than of good. Genius like mine must needs have with it manifold bad. "I have in me the germ of every crime." I have no desire to destroy these germs. I should be glad indeed to have them develop into a ravaging disease. Something in this dreadful confusion would then give way. My wooden heart and my soul would cry out in the darkness less heavily, less bitterly.

They want something—they know not what.

I give them poison.

They snatch it and eat it hungrily.

Then they are not so hungry. They become quieter.

The ravaging disease soothes them to sleep—it descends on them like rain in the autumn.

When I hurry over my sand and barrenness my vivid passions come to me—or when I sit and look at the horizon. When I walk slowly I consider calmly the question of how much evil I should need to kill off my finer feelings, to poison thoroughly this soul of unrest and this wooden heart so that they would never more be conscious of too-brilliant lights, and to make myself over into a quite different creature.

A little evil would do—a little of a fine, good quality.

I should like a man to come (it is always a man, have you ever noticed?—whatever one contemplates when one is of womankind and young). I should like a man to come, I said calmly to myself to-day as I walked slowly over my barrenness—a perfect villain to come and fascinate me and lead me with strong, gentle allurements to what would be technically termed my ruin. And as the world views such things it would be my ruin. But as I view such things it would not be ruin. It would be a new lease on life.

Yes, I should like a man to come—any man so that he is strong and thoroughly a villain, and so that he fascinates me. Particularly he must fascinate me. There must be no falling in love about it. I doubt if I could fascinate him, but I should ask him quite humbly to lead me to my ruin.

I have never yet seen the man who would not readily respond to such an appeal.

This villain would be no exception.

I would then jerk my life out of this Nothingness by the roots. Farewell, a long farewell, I would say. Then I would go forth with the man to my ruin. The man would be bad to his heart's core. And after living but a short time with him my shy, sensitive soul would be irretrievably poisoned and polluted. The defilement of so sacred and beautiful a thing as marriage is surely the darkest evil that can come to a life. And so everything within me that had turned toward that too-bright light would then drink deep of the lees of death.

The thirst of this incessant unrest and longing, this weariness of self, would be quenched completely.

My life would be like fertile soil planted thickly with rank wild mustard. On every square inch of soil there would be a dozen sprouts of wild mustard. There would be no room—no room at all—for an anemone to grow. If one should start up, instantly it would be choked and overrun with wild mustard. But no anemone would start up.

My life now is a life of pain and revolt.

My life darkened and partly killed would be more than content to drift along with the current.

Oh, it would be a rest!

The Christians sing, there is rest for the weary, on the other side of Jordan, where the tree of life is blooming. But that rest, of course, is for the Christians. My rest will have to come on this side of Jordan. Let the impress of a thoroughly evil and strong man be stamped upon my inner life, and I am convinced there would come a wonderful settled quiet over it. Its spirit would be broken. It would rest. Why not? I have no virtue-sense. Nothing to me is of any consequence except to be rid of this unrest and pain. Yes, surely I might rest.

The coming of the man-devil would bring rest. But I am fool enough to think that marriage—the real marriage—is possible for me!

This other thing is within the reach of every one—of fools and geniuses alike—and of all that come between.

And so I want a fascinating wicked man to come and make me positively, rather than negatively, wicked. I feel a terrific wave of utter weariness. My life lies fallow. I am tired of sitting here. The sand and barrenness is gray with age. And I am gray with age.

Happiness—the red of the sunset sky—is the intensest desire of my life.

But I will grasp eagerly anything else that is offered me—*anything*.

The poisoning of my soul—the passing of my unrest—would rouse my mental power. My genius would receive a wonderful impetus from it. You would marvel, good world, at the things I should write. Not that they would be exalted—not that they would surge upward. Do men gather grapes of thorns or figs of thistles? But they would be marvels of fire and intensity. I should no longer exhaust much of my energy in grinding, grinding within. The things that would come of the thorns and thistles would excite your astonishment and admiration, though they be not grapes and figs.

And as for me—the real me—the creature imbued with a spirit of intense femininity, with a spirit of an intense sense of Love—with a spirit like that of the Magdalene who loved too much, with the very soul of unrest and Nothingness—this thing would vanish swiftly into oblivion, and I should go down a dark world and feel not.

ONE of the remarkable points about my life is that it is so completely, hopelessly alone—a lonely, lonely life. This book of mine contains but one character—myself.

There is also the Devil—as a possibility.

And there is also the anemone lady—my dearest beloved—as a memory.

I have read books that were written to portray but one character, and there were various people brought in to help in the portraying. But my one friend is one, and there is no person who enters into my inner life in the very least. I am always alone. I might mingle with people intimately every hour of my life—still I should be alone.

Always alone—alone.

Not even a God to worship.

How do I bear this? How do I get through the days and days?

And, oh, when it all comes over me, what frightful rage—what long agony of my breaking heart—what utter woe!

When the stars shine down upon me with cold hatred; when miles and miles of barrenness stretch out around me and envelop me in their weary, weary Nothingness; when the wind blows over me like the breath of a vicious giant; when the ugly, ugly sun radiates centuries of hard, heavy bitterness around me from its stinging rays; when the sky maddens me with its cold, careless blue; when the rivers that are flowing over the earth send echoes to me of their hateful voices; when I hear wild geese honking in bitter wailing melody; when bristling edges of jagged rocks cut sharply into my tired life; when drops of rain fall on me and pierce me like steel points; when the voices in the air shriek little-minded malice in my ears; when the green of Nature is the green of spitefulness and cruelty; when the red, red of the setting sun burns and consumes me with its horrid feverish effervescence; when I feel the all-hatred of the Universe for its poor little earth-bugs: then it is that I approach nearest to Rest.

The softnesses are my Unrest.

I do not want those bitter things.

But I must have them if I would rest.
I want the softnesses and I want Rest!
Oh, dear faint soul, it is hard—hard for us.
We are sick with loneliness.

26 MARCH.

NOW and again I have torturing glimpses of a Paradise. And I feel my soul in its pain every moment of my life. Otherwise, how gladly would I deny the existence of a soul and a life to come!

For my soul is beset with Nothingness, and the Paradise that shows itself is not for me.

28 MARCH.

HATRED, after all, is the easiest thing of all to bear.

If you have been forgotten by the one who must have made you, and if you have been left alone of human beings all your life—all your nineteen years—then, when at last you see some one looking toward you with beautiful eyes, and extending to you a beautiful hand, and showing you a beautiful heart wherein is just a little of beautiful sympathy for you—for you—oh, that is harder than anything to bear. Harder than the loneliness and the bitterness—and the tears are nearer and nearer.

But one would be hurt often, often for the sake of the beautiful things. Yes, one would gladly be hurt long and often.

I shall never forget how it was with me when I first saw the beautiful eyes of my dearest anemone lady when they were looking gently—at me—and the beautiful hand, and the beautiful heart.

The awakening of my racked soul is hardly more heavily laden with passion and pain. I shall never forget.

Though I feel away from her also, she is the only one out of all to look gently at me.

Let me writhe and falter with pain; let me go mad—but oh,

worldful of people—for the love of your God—give me out of this seething darkness only one beautiful human hand to touch mine with love, one beautiful human heart to know the aching sad loneliness of mine, one beautiful, human soul to mingle with mine in long, long Rest.

Oh, for a human being, my soul wails—a human being to love me!

Oh, to know—just once—what it is to be loved!

Nineteen years without one faint shadow of love is mouldy, crumbling age—is gray with the dust of centuries.

How long have I lived?

How long must I live?

I am shrieking at you, cold, stupid world.

Oh, the long, long waiting!

The millions of human beings!

I am a human being and there is no one—no one—no one.

Who can know this that has not felt it? You do not know—you can not know.

Surely I do not ask too much. But whether or not it is too much I can not go through the years without it—oh, I can not!

You have lived your nineteen years, fine world, and you have lived through some after years.

But in your nineteen years there was some one to love you.

It is that that counts.

Since you have had that some one, in your nineteen years, can you understand what life is to me—me—in my loneliness?

My wailing, waiting soul burns with but one desire: *to be loved—oh, to be loved.*

29 MARCH.

I AM making the world my confessor in this Portrayal. My mind is fairly bursting with egotism and pain, and in writing this I find a merciful outlet. I have become fond of my Portrayal. Often I lay my forehead and my lips caressingly upon the pages.

And I wish to let you know that there is in existence a genius—an unhappy genius, a genius starving in Montana in the barrenness—but still a genius. I am a creature the like of which you have never before happened upon. You have never suspected that there is such a person. I know that there is not such another. As I said in the beginning, the world contains not my parallel.

I am a fantasy—an absurdity—a genius!

Had I been one of the beasts that perish I had been likewise a fantasy. I think I should have been a small animal composite of a pig, a leopard, and a skunk: an animal that I fancy would be uncanny to look upon but admirable for a pet.

However, I am not one of the beasts that perish.

I am human.

That is another remarkable point.

I have heard persons say they can hardly believe I am quite human.

I am the most human creature that ever was placed on the earth. The geniuses are always more human than the herd. Almost a perfection of humanness is reached in me. This by itself makes me extraordinary. The rarest thing in the world, I find, is the quality of humanness.

Humanity and humaneness are much less rare.

"It is a brave thing to understand something of what we see." Indeed it is. An exceeding brave thing. The one who said that had surely gone out on the highways and byways and found how little he could understand.

To understand oneself is not so brave a thing. To go in among the hidden gray shadows of the deep things is a fool's errand. It is not from choice that I do it. No one carries a millstone around her neck from choice. When I see what is among the hidden gray shadows—when I see a vision of *Myself*—I am seized with a strange, sick terror.

A fool's errand—but one that I must need go—and for that matter I myself am a fool.

Yet to know oneself well is a rare fine art.

I analyze myself now. I analyzed myself when I was three years old.

The only difference is that at the age of three I was not aware that I analyzed. It is true, that is a great difference. Now I know that I am analyzing at nineteen, and now I know that I analyzed at three.

And at the age of nineteen I know that I am a genius.

A genius who does not know that he is a genius is no genius. A drunken man might stagger up to a piano and accidentally play music that vibrates to the soul—that touches upon the mysteries. But he does not know his power, and he is no genius, though men awaken and go mad therefrom.

I know that I am a genius more than any genius that has lived.

I have a feeling that the world will never know this.

And as I think of it I wonder if angels are not weeping somewhere because of it.

31 MARCH.

She only said: "My life is dreary,
He cometh not," she said;
She said, "I am aweary, aweary.
I would that I were dead!"

ALL day long this heart-sickening song of Mariana has been reeling and swimming in my brain. I awoke with it early in the morning, and it is still with me now in the lateness. I wondered at times during the day why that very gentle and devilishly persistent refrain did not drive me insane or send me into convulsions. I tried vainly to fix my mind on a book. I began reading "Mill on the Floss," but that weird poem was not to be foiled. It bewitched my brain. Now, as I write, I hear twenty voices chanting in a sad minor key—twenty voices that fill my brain with sound to the bursting point. "He cometh not—he cometh not—he cometh not." "That I were dead"—"I am aweary, aweary,"—"that I were dead—that I were dead." "He cometh not—that I were dead."

It is maddening in that it is set sublimely to the music of my own life.

Now that I have written it I can hope that it may leave me. If it follows me through the night, and if I awake to another day of it the cords of my overworked mind will surely break.

But let me thank the kind Devil.
It is leaving me now!
It is as if tons were lifted from my brain.

2 April.

HOW can any one bring a child into the world and not wrap it round with a certain wondrous tenderness that will stay with it always!

There are persons whose souls have never entered into them.

My mother has some fondness for me—for my body because it came of hers. That is nothing—nothing.

A hen loves its egg.

A hen!

3 April.

THIS evening in the slow-deepening dusk I sat by my window and spent an hour in passionate conversation with the Devil. I fancied I sat, with my hands folded and my feet crossed, on an ugly but comfortable red velvet sofa in some nondescript room.

And the fascinating man-devil was seated near in a frail willow chair.

He had willingly come to pass the time of day with me. He was in a good-humored mood, and I amused and interested him. And for myself, I was extremely glad to see the Devil sitting there and felt vividly as always. But I sat quietly enough.

The fascinating man-devil has fascinating steel-gray eyes, and they looked at me with every variety of glance—from quizzical to tender.

It were easy—oh, how easy—to follow those eyes to the earth's ends.

The Devil leaned back in the frail willow chair and looked at me.

"And now that I am here, Mary MacLane," he said, "what

would you?"

"I want you to marry me," I replied at once. "And I want it more than ever anything was wanted since the world began."

"So? I am flattered," said the Devil, and smiled gently, enchantingly.

At that smile I was ravished and transported, and a spasm of some rare emotion thrilled all the little nerves in me from my heels to my forehead. And yet the smile was not for me but rather somewhat at my expense.

"But," he went on, "you must know it is not my custom to marry women."

"I am sure it is not," I agreed, "and I do not ask to be peculiarly favored. Anything that you may give me, however little, will constitute marriage for me."

"And would marriage itself be so small a thing?" asked the Devil.

"Marriage," I said, "would be a great, oh, a wonderful thing, and the most beautiful of all. I want what is good according to my lights, and because I am a genius my lights are many and far-reaching."

"What do your lights tell you?" the man-devil inquired.

"They tell me this: that nothing in the world matters unless love is with it, and if love is with it and it seems to the virtuous a barren and infamous thing, still—because of the love—it partakes of the very highest."

"And have you the courage of your convictions?" he said.

"If you offered me," I replied, "that which to the blindly virtuous seems the worst possible thing, it would yet be for me the red, red line on the sky, my heart's desire, my life, my rest. You are the Devil. I have fallen in love with you."

"I believe you have," said the Devil. "And how does it feel to be in love?"

Sitting composedly on the ugly red velvet sofa, with my hands folded and my feet crossed, I attempted to define that wonderful feeling.

"It feels," I said, "as if sparks of fire and ice crystals ran riot in my veins with my blood; as if a thousand pinpoints pierced my flesh, and every other point a point of pleasure, and every other point a point of pain; as if my heart were laid to rest in a bed of velvet and cotton-wool but kept awake by sweet violin arias; as if milk and honey and the blossoms of the cherry flowed into my stomach and then vanished utterly; as if strange, beautiful worlds lay spread out before my eyes, alternately in dazzling light and complete darkness with chaotic rapidity; as if orris-root were sprinkled in the folds of my brain; as if sprigs of dripping-wet sweet-fern were stuck inside my hot linen collar; as if—well, you know," I ended suddenly.

"Very good," said the Devil. "You are in love. And you say you are in love with me."

"Oh, with you!" I exclaimed with suppressed violence. The effort to suppress this violence cost me pounds of nerve-power. But I kept my hands still quietly folded and my feet crossed, and it was a triumph of self-control. "I want you to marry me," I added despairingly.

"And you think," he inquired, "that apart from the opinion of the wise world, it would be a suitable marriage?"

"A suitable marriage!" I exclaimed. "I hate a suitable marriage! No, it would not be suitable. It would be Bohemian, outlandish, adorable!"

The Devil smiled.

This time the smile was for me. And, oh, the long, old, overpowering enchantment of the smile of steel-gray eyes!—the steel-gray eyes of the Devil!

It is one of those things that one remembers.

"You are a beautifully frank, little feminine creature," he said. "Frankness is in these days a lost art."

"Yes, I am beautifully frank," I replied. "Out of countless millions of the Devil's anointed I am one to acknowledge myself."

"But withal you are not true," said the man-devil.

"I am a liar," I answered.

"You are a liar, surely," he said, "but you stay with your lies. To stay with anything is Truth."

"It is so," I replied, "Nevertheless I am false as woman can be."

"But you know what you want."

"Oh, yes," I said, "I know what I want. I want you to marry me."

"And why?"

"Because I love you."

"That seems an excellent reason, certainly," said the Devil.

"I want to be happy for once in my life," I said. "I have never been happy. And if I could be happy once for one gold day, I should be satisfied, and I should have that to remember in the long years."

"And you are a strangely pathetic little animal," said the Devil.

"I am pathetic," I said. I clasped my hands very tightly. "I know that I am pathetic: and for this reason I am the most terribly pathetic of all in the world."

"Poor little Mary MacLane!" said the Devil. He leaned toward me. He looked at me with those strange, wonderfully tender, divine steel-gray eyes. "Poor little Mary MacLane!" he said again in a voice that was like the Gray Dawn. And the eyes—the glance of the steel-gray eyes entered into me and thrilled me through and through. It frightened and soothed me. It racked and comforted me. It ravished me with inconceivable gentleness so that I bent my head down and sobbed as I breathed.

"Don't you know, you little thing," said the man-devil, softly-compassionate, "your life will be very hard for you always—harder when you are happy than when you go in Nothingness?"

"I know—I know. Nevertheless I want to be happy," I sobbed. I felt a rush of an old thick, heavy anguish. "It is day after day. It is week after week. It is month after month. It is year after year. It is only time going and going. There is no joy. There is no lightness of heart. It is only the passing of days. I am young and all alone. Always I have been alone: when I was five and lay in the damp grass and tortured myself to keep back tears; and through the long, cold, lonely years till now—and now all the torture does not keep back the tears. There is no one—nothing—to help me bear it. It is more than pathetic when one is nineteen in all young, new feeling and sees Nothing anywhere—except long, dark, lonely years behind her and before her. No one that loves me and long, long years."

I stopped. The gray eyes were fixed on me. Oh, they were

the steel-gray eyes!—and they had a look in them. The long, bitter pageant of my Nothingness mingled with this look and the coming together of these was like the joining of two halves.

I do not know which brings me the deeper pain—the loneliness and weariness of my sand and barrenness, or the look in the steel-gray eyes. But as always I would gladly leave all and follow the eyes to the world's end. They are like the sun's setting. And they are like the pale, beautiful stars. And they are like the shadows of earth and sky that come together in the dark.

"Why," asked the Devil, "are you in love with me?"

"You know so much—so much," I answered. "I think it must be that. The wisdom of the spheres is in your brain. And so, then, you must understand me. Because no one understands all these smouldering feelings my greatest agony is. You must need know the very finest of them. And your eyes! Oh, it's no matter why I'm in love with you. It's enough that I am. And if you married me I would make you happier than you are."

"I am not happy at all," said the man-devil. "I am merely contented."

"Contentment," I said, "in place of Happiness, is a horrid feeling. Not one of your countless advocates loves you. They all serve you faithfully and well, but with it all they hate you. Always people hate their tyrant. You are my tyrant, but I love you absorbingly, madly. Happiness for me would be to live with you and see you made happy by the overwhelming flood of my love."

"It interests me," he said. "You are a most interesting feminine philosopher—and your philosophy is after my own heart, in its lack of virtue. It is to be hoped you are not 'intellectual,' which is an unpardonable trait."

"Indeed, I am not," I replied. "Intellectual people are detestable. They have pale faces and bad stomachs and bad livers, and if they are women their corsets are sure to be too tight, and probably black, and if they are men they are soft, which is worse. And they never by any chance know what it means to walk all day in the rain, or to roll around on the ground in the dirt. And, above all, they never fall in love with the Devil."

"They are tiresome," the Devil agreed. "If I were to marry you how long would you be happy?"

"For three days."

"You are wise," he said. "You are wonderfully wise in some things, though you are still very young."

"I am wise," I answered. "Being of womankind and nineteen years, I am more than ready to give up absolutely everything that is good in the world's sight, though they are contemptible things enough in my own, for love. All for love. Therefore I am wise. Also I am a fool."

"Why are you a fool?"

"Because I am a genius."

"Your logic is good logic," said the Devil.

"My logic—oh, I don't care anything about logic," I said with sudden complete weariness. I felt buried and wrapped round and round in weariness. Everything lost its color. Everything turned cold.

"At this moment," said the Devil, "you feel as if you cared for nothing at all. But if I chose I could bring about a transfiguration. I could kiss your soul into Paradise."

I answered, "Yes," without emotion.

"An hour," said the Devil, "is not very long. But we know it is long enough to suffer in, and go mad in, and live in, and be happy in. And the world contains a great many hours. Now I am leaving you. It is likely that I may never come again, and it is likely that I may come again."

It all vanished. I still sat by my window in the gloom. "It is dreary," I said.

But yes. The world contains a great many hours.

4 APRIL.

I HAVE asked for bread, sometimes, and I have been given a stone.

Oh, it is a bitter thing—oh, it is piteous, piteous!

I find that I am not far apart from human beings I can still be crushed, wounded, stunned, by the attitude of human beings.

Today I looked for human-kindness, and I was given coldness. I repelled human beings.

I asked for bread and I was given a stone.

Oh, it is bitter—bitter.

Oh, is there a thing in the wide world more bitter?

God, where are you! I am crushed, wounded, stunned—and, oh—I am alone!

10 April.

I HAVE a sense of humor that partakes of the divine in life—for there are things even in this chaotic irony that are divine. My genius is not divine. My patheticness is not divine. My philosophy is not divine, nor my originality, nor my audacity of thought. These are peculiarly of the earth. But my sense of humor—

It is humor that is far too deep to admit of laughter. It is humor that makes my heart melt with a high, unequaled sense of pleasure and ripple down through my body like old yellow wine.

A rare tone in a person's voice, a densely wrathful expression in a pair of slate-colored eyes, a fine, fine shade of comparison and contrast between a word in a conversation and an angleworm pattern in a calico dressing-jacket—these are things that make me conscious of divine emotion.

One day last summer an Italian peddler-woman stopped at the back door and rested herself. I stood in the doorway, and the peddler-woman and I talked. She had a dirty white handkerchief tied over her head—as all Italian peddler-women do—and she had a telescope valise filled with garters, and hairpins, and soap, and combs, and pencils, and china buttons on blue cards, and bean-shooters, and tacks, and dream-books, and mouth-organs, and green glass beads, and jews-harps. There is something fascinating about a peddler-woman's telescope valise. This peddler-woman wore a black satine wrapper and an ancient cape. She said that she would like to stop and rest a while, and I told her she might. I had always wanted to talk to a peddler-woman, and my mother never would allow one in the house.

"Is it nice to be a peddler?" I asked her.

"It ain't bad," replied the peddler-woman.

"Do you make a great deal of money?" I next inquired.

"Sometime I do, and sometime I don't," said the woman. She spoke with an accent that, while it sounded Italian, still showed unmistakably that she had lived in Butte.

"Well, do you make just enough to live on, or have you saved some money?" I asked.

"I got four hundred dollar in the bank," she replied. "I been peddlin' eight year."

"Eight years of tramping around in all kinds of weather," I said. "Your philosophy must be peripatetic, too. Haven't you ever had rheumatism in your knees?"

"I got rheumatism in every joint in my body," said the woman. "I have to lay off, sometime."

"Have you a husband?" I wished to know.

"I had a man—oh, yes," said the peddler-woman.

"And where is he?"

"Back home—in Italy."

"Why doesn't he come out here and work for you?" I asked.

"Yes, w'y don't he?" said the woman. "Dat-a man, he's dem lucky w'en he can get enough to eat—he is."

"Why don't you send him some money to pay his way out, since you've saved so much?" I inquired.

"Holy God!" said the peddler-woman. "I work hard for dat-a money. I save ev'ry cent. I ain't go'n now to t'row it away—I ain't. Dat-a man, he's all right w'ere he is—he is."

"What did you marry him for?" I asked.

The peddler-woman looked at me with that look which seems to convey the information that curiosity once killed a cat.

"What for?" I persisted—"for love?"

"I marry him w'en I was young girl. And he was young, too."

"Yes—but what did you do it for? Was he awfully nice, and did he say awfully sweet things to you?"

"He was dem sweet—oh, yes," said the peddler-woman. She grinned. "And I was young."

"And you liked it when you were young and he was sweet, didn't you?"

"Yes, I guess so. I was young," she answered.

The fact that one is young seems to imply—in the Italian

peddler mind—a lacking in some essential points.

"And don't you like your man now?" I asked.

"Dat-a man, he's all right, in Italy he is," replied the woman.

"Well," I observed, "if I had a man who had been dem sweet once, when I had been young, but who was not sweet any more, I think I should leave him in Italy, too."

"You'll git a man some day soon," said the peddler-woman.

I was interested to know that.

"They all do—oh, yes," she said. "But you likely to be better off peddlin', I tell you."

"Yes, I think it would be amusing to be a peddler for a while," I said. "But I should want the man, too, as long as he was dem sweet."

The peddler-woman picked up the telescope valise.

"Yes," she remarked, "a man, he's sweet two days, tree days, then—holy God! he never work, he git-a drunk, he make-a rough-house, he raise hell."

The peddler-woman nodded at me and limped out of the yard. The telescope valise was heavy. When she walked every muscle in her body, seemed to be pressed into the service. She had a heavy, solid look. She seemed as though she might weigh three hundred pounds, though she was not large. The afternoon sun shone down brightly on her dirty white handkerchief, on her brown comely face, on her brown brass-ringed hands, on her black satine wrapper, on her ancient cape.

As I watched her out of sight I thought to myself: "Two days, tree days, then—holy God! he never work, he git-a drunk, he make-a rough-house, he raise hell."

I was conscious of an intense humor that was so far beyond laughter that it was too deep even for tears. But I felt tears vaguely as I watched the peddler-woman limping up the road.

It was not pathos. It was humor—humor. My emotion was one of vivid pleasure—pleasure at the sight of the woman, and at the telescope valise, and at her conversation supplemented by my own.

This emotion is divine, and I can not grasp it.

As I looked after the Italian peddler-woman it came to me

with sudden force that the earth is only the earth, but that it is touched here and there brilliantly with divine fingers.

Long and often as I've sat in intense silent passion and gazed at the red, red sunset sky, I have never then felt this sense of the divine.

It comes only through humor.

It comes only with things like an Italian peddler-woman in a black satine wrapper and an ancient cape.

My soul—how heavily it goes.

Life is a journeying up a spring-time hill. And at the top we wonder why we are there. Have mercy on me, I implore in a dull idea that the journey is so long—so long, and a human being is less than an atom.

The solid, heavy figure of an Italian peddler-woman with a telescope valise, limping away in the afternoon sunshine, is more convincing of the Things that Are than would be the sound of the wailing of legions of lost souls, could it be heard.

For the world must be amused.

And the world's wind listeth as it bloweth.

11 APRIL.

I WRITE a great many letters to the dear anemone lady. I send some of them to her and others I keep to read myself. I like to read letters that I have written—particularly that I have written to her.

This is a letter that I wrote two days ago to my one friend:

"To you:—

"And don't you know, my dearest, my friendship with you contains other things? It contains infatuation, and worship, and bewitchment, and idolatry, and a tiny altar in my soul-chamber whereon is burning sweet incense in a little dish of blue and gold.

"Yes, all of these.

"My life is made up of many outpourings. All the outpourings have one point of coming-together. You are the point of coming-together. There is no other.

"You are the anemone lady.

"You are the one whom I may love.

"To think that the world contains one beautiful human being for me to love!

"It is wonderful.

"My life is longing for the sight of you. My senses are aching for lack of an anemone to diffuse itself among them.

"A year ago, when you were in the high school, often I used to go over there when you would be going home, so that my life could be made momentarily replete by the sight of you. You didn't know I was there—only a few times when I spoke to you.

"And now it is that I remember you.

"Oh, my dearest—you are the only one in the world!

"We are two women. You do not love me, but I love you.

"You have been wonderfully, beautifully kind to me.

"You are the only one who has ever been kind to me.

"There is something delirious in this—something of the nameless quantity.

"It is old grief and woe to live nineteen years and to remember no person ever to have been kind. But what is it—do you think?—at the end of nineteen years, to come at last upon one who is wonderfully, beautifully kind!

"Those persons who have had some one always to be kind to them can never remotely imagine how this feels.

"Sometimes in these spring days when I walk miles down into the country to the little wet gulch of the sweet-flags, I wonder why it is that this thing does not make me happy. 'She is wonderfully, beautifully kind,' I say to myself—'and she is the anemone lady. She is *wondrously* kind, and though she's gone, nothing can ever change that.'

"But I am not happy.

"Oh, my one friend—what is the matter with me? What is this feeling? Why am I not happy?

"But how can you know?

"You are beautiful.

"I am a small, vile creature.

"Always I awake to this fact when I think of the anemone lady.

"I am not good.

"But you are kind to me—you are kind to me—you are

kind to me.

"You have written me two letters.

"The anemone lady came down from her high places and wrote me two letters.

"It is said that God is somewhere. It may be so.

"But God has never come down from his high places to write me two letters.

"Dear—do you see?—you are the only one in the world.

"MARY MACLANE."

12 APRIL.

OH, THE dreariness, the Nothingness!

Day after day—week after week,—it is dull and gray and weary.

It is *dull*, DULL, DULL!

No one loves me the least in the world.

"My life is dreary—he cometh not."

I am unhappy—unhappy.

It rains. The blue sky is weeping. But it is not weeping because I am unhappy.

I hate the blue sky, and the rain, and the wet ground, and everything. This morning I walked far away over the sand, and these things made me think they loved me—and that I loved them. But they fooled me. Everything fools me. I am a fool.

No one loves me. There are people here. But no one loves me—no one understands—no one cares.

It is I and the barrenness. It is I—young and all alone.

Pitiful Heaven!—but no, Heaven is not pitiful.

Heaven also has fooled me, more than once.

There is something for every one that I have ever known—some tender thing. But what is there for me? What have I to remember out of the long years?

The blue sky is weeping, but not for me. The rain is persistent and heavy as damnation. It falls on my Mind and it maddens my mind. It falls on my soul and it hurts my soul.—Everything hurts my soul.—It falls on my heart and it warps the wood in my heart.

Of womankind and nineteen years, a philosopher of the peripatetic school, a thief, a genius, a liar, and a fool—and unhappy, and filled with anguish and hopeless despair. What is my life? Oh, what is there for me!

There has always been Nothing. There will always be Nothing.

There was a miserable, damnable, wretched, lonely childhood. Itself has passed, but the pain of it has not passed. The pain of it is with me and is added to the pain of now. It is pain that never lets itself be forgotten. The pain of the childhood was the pain of Nothing. The pain of now is the pain of Nothing. Oh, the pathetic burlesque-tragedy of Nothing!

It is burlesque, but it is none the less tragedy. It is tragedy that eats its way inward.

It is only I and the sand and barrenness.

I have never a tender thing in my life. The sand and barrenness has never a grass-blade.

I want a human being to love me. I have need of it. I am starving to death for lack of it.

Bitterest salt tears surge upward—sobs are shaking themselves out from the depths. Oh, the salt is bitter. I might lay me down and weep all day and all night—and the salt would grow more bitter and more bitter.

But life in its Nothingness is more bitter still.

It is burlesque-tragedy that is the most tragic of all.

It is an inward dying that never ends. It is the bitterness of death added to the bitterness of life.

What hell is there like that of one weak little human being placed on the earth—and left *alone?*

There are people who live and enjoy. But my soul and I—we find life too bitter, and too heavy to carry alone. Too bitter, and too heavy.

Oh, that I and my soul might perish at this moment, forever!

13 April.

I AM sitting writing out on my sand and barrenness. The sky is pale and faded now in the west, but a few minutes ago there was the same old-time, always-new miracle of roses and gold, and glints and gleams of silver and green, and a river in vermilions and purples—and lastly the dear, the beautiful: the red, red line.

There also are heavy black shadows.

I have given my heart into the keeping of this.

And still, as always, I look at it—and feel it all with thrilling passion—and await the Devil's coming.

L'ENVOI

28 October 1901.

AND so there you have my Portrayal. It is the record of three months of Nothingness. Those three months are very like the three months that preceded them, to be sure, and the three that followed them—and like all the months that have come and gone with me, since time was. There is never anything different; nothing ever happens.

Now I will send my Portrayal into the wise wide world. It may stop short at the publisher; or it may fall still-born from the press; or it may go farther, indeed, and be its own undoing.

That's as may be.

I will send it.

What else is there for me, if not this book?

And, oh, that some one may understand it!

—I am not good. I am not virtuous. I am not sympathetic. I am not generous. I am merely and above all a creature of intense passionate feeling. I feel—everything. It is my genius. It burns me like fire.—

My Portrayal in its analysis and egotism and bitterness will surely be of interest to some. Whether to that one alone who may understand it; or to some who have themselves been left alone; or to those three whom I, on three dreary days, asked for bread, and who each gave me a stone—and whom I do not forgive (for that is the bitterest thing of all): it may be to all of these.

But none of them, nor any one, can know the feeling made of relief and pain and despair that comes over me at the thought of sending all this to the wise, wide world. It is bits of my wooden heart broken off and given away. It is strings of amber beads taken from the fair neck of my soul. It is shining little gold coins from out of my mind's red leather purse. It is my little old life-tragedy.

It means everything to me.

Do you see?—it means *everything* to me.

It will amuse you. It will arouse your interest. It will stir your curiosity. Some sorts of persons will find it ridiculous. It will puzzle you.

But am I to suppose that it will also awaken compassion in cool, indifferent hearts? And will the sand and barrenness look so unspeakably gray and dreary to coldly critical eyes as to mine? And shall my bitter little story fall easily and comfortably upon undisturbed ears, and linger for an hour, and be forgotten?

Will the wise wide world itself give me in my outstretched hand a stone?

THE END

Frontispiece of *My Friend Annabel Lee* (1903)

Selections from *MY FRIEND ANNABEL LEE*

PROVERBS

"What's a bird in the hand worth?" said I.
"A pound of cure," said my friend Annabel Lee.
"What does a stitch in time save?" said I.
"Two in the bush," said my friend Annabel Lee.
"Where does charity begin?" said I.
"Betwixt the cup and the lip," said my friend Annabel Lee.
"What may a cat look at?" said I.
"The broth," said my friend Annabel Lee.
"What does many a mickle make?" said I.
"A multitude of sins," said my friend Annabel Lee.
"What do too many cooks spoil?" said I.
"Us all," said my friend Annabel Lee.
"Whom does conscience make cowards of?" said I.
"Dead men and fools," said my friend Annabel Lee.
"What is it that has no turning?" said I.
"A full stomach," said my friend Annabel Lee.
"What fortifies a stout heart?" said I.
"A stitch in time," said my friend Annabel Lee.
"What does money make?" said I.
"An ill wind," said my friend Annabel Lee.
"What will the pounds do if you take care of the pence?" said I.
"Come home to roost," said my friend Annabel Lee.
"Where is there many a slip?" said I.
"Where angels fear to tread," said my friend Annabel Lee.
"What's sharper than a serpent's tooth?" said I.
"The pen," said my friend Annabel Lee.
"What's mightier than the sword?" said I.
"A rich man," said my friend Annabel Lee.
"What makes the mare go?" said I.
"A fool and his money," said my friend Annabel Lee.
"What should they do who live in glass houses?" said I.
"Draw down the blinds," said my friend Annabel Lee.
"What's a man's castle?" said I.

"The devil's workshop," said my friend Annabel Lee.
"What's better to do than to break?" said I.
"Rob Peter," said my friend Annabel Lee.
"What's the wind tempered to?" said I.
"The camel's back," said my friend Annabel Lee.
"What do many hands make?" said I.
"A shorn lamb," said my friend Annabel Lee.
"What can't you make out of a pig's ear?" said I.
"A gift-horse," said my friend Annabel Lee.
"What should you never look in the mouth?" said I.
"A silk purse," said my friend Annabel Lee.
"What's half a loaf better than?" said I.
"Chickens before they are hatched," said my friend
Annabel Lee.

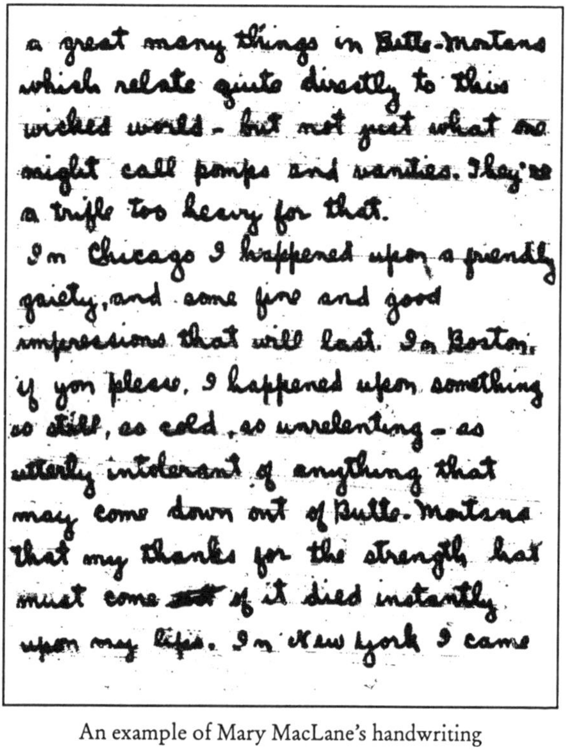
a great many things in Butte-Montana
which relate quite directly to this
wicked world - but not just what one
might call pomps and vanities. They're
a trifle too heavy for that.
In Chicago I happened upon a friendly
gaiety, and some fine and good
impressions that will last. In Boston,
if you please, I happened upon something
so still, so cold, so unrelenting - so
utterly intolerant of anything that
may come down out of Butte-Montana
that my thanks for the strength that
must come ~~out~~ of it died instantly
upon my lips. In New York I came

An example of Mary MacLane's handwriting

THE GOLDEN RIPPLE

My friend Annabel Lee and I are similar to each other in a few, few ways. Daily we contemplate together a great, blank wall built up of dull, blue stones. It stands before us and we can not get over it, for it is too high; neither can we walk around it, for it is too long; and we can not go through it, for it is solid and very thick. It is directly across the road. We have both come but a short way on the road—so short that we can easily look back over our course to the point where we started. We did not walk together from there, but we have met each other now before the great, blank wall of blue stones.

We have stopped here, for we can not go on. I wonder and conjecture much about the wall, and my friend Annabel Lee regards it sometimes with interest and sometimes with none.

And, times, we forget all about the wall and merely sit and rest in the shade it casts, or walk back on the road, or in the grass about it, or pluck a few wild sweet berries from the stunted wayside briers.

And, too, when a thunder storm comes up and the air is full of wind and rain slanting and whistling about us, we crouch close against the base of the wall, and we do not become so wet as we should were there no wall.

But that is only when the wind is from beyond it.

When the wind with its flood of rain comes toward us as we crouch by the wall we are beaten and drenched and buffeted and driven hard against theat cold, blue surface. And the ragged edges of the rocks make bruises on our foreheads.

Some days we become exceeding weary with looking at the great blank wall—and with having looked at it already for many a day, and many a day.

"It is so big and so thick," I say.

"It is so long," says my friend Annabel Lee.

To all appearances we have gone as far upon the road as we ever can go. We can not get over the wall of blue stones—and we can not walk round—and we can not go through. There is nothing to indicate that it will ever be removed.

The field for conjecture as to what lies on the other side of the road is so vast that we do not venture to conjecture.

But we have talked often and madly of the wall itself.

"Perhaps," I say, "it is that the wall is placed here before our eyes to hide from us our limitations."

"Perhaps," says my friend Annabel Lee, "it is that the wall itself is our limitations."

Which, if it is true, is very damnable.

For though human beings have done some divine things they have never gone beyond their limitations.

The blue in the stones of the wall is not a dark blue, but it is very cold. It is the color that is called stone blue.

It never changes.

The sun and the shade look alike upon it; and the wet rain does not brighten it; neither do thick clouds of dust make it dull.

It is stone blue.

Except for this:

Once in a number of days, in fair weather or foul, there will come upon the wide blankness a rippling like gold.

It lingers a second and vanishes—and appears again. And then it's gone until another time.

How tender, how lovely, how bright is the golden ripple against the cold, cold blue!

It is come and gone in a minute.

We do not know its coming or its going.

But while we see it our hearts beat high and fast.

"It may be," I say when it is gone, "that this golden ripple will show us some way to get beyond the wall where things are divine."

"It may be," says my friend Annabel Lee, "that the golden ripple will show us something divine among these few things on this side of the wall."

Selections from *I, MARY MACLANE*

A HUMAN PREROGATIVE

It is a quiet deep of night. A bell has just tolled two.

I am clothed in cool bedroom negligées and a softening sweetness of cold cream, from head to foot.

I am tranquil for today I had a walk that made me feel Sincere and Safe.

It is a comforting feeling: it is like a beef-sandwich. It was a long walk southeast of Butte along an outskirting road where I used often to walk when I was sixteen—a broad gray desert. It was the same sand and barrenness. It was bare and withered as if a giant coyote had picked its rocky ribs.

The day was windy and dusty. The sunshine was thick and sweet and heavy like floating honey. The dust that blew against the white of my neck was like ground glass.

My feet ached as I walked.

My shoes were Cuban-heeled thick-soled pumps of corded silk, a kind easy to walk in. But the same feet which once readily bore me seven miles along that road ache now at three. All of me ached as I walked along. I cursed desultorily with a smooth whispered flow of curses, because the circumstances seemed to demand it. But I loved the walk—even the more for my tired feet and my aching knees and my irking drooping shoulders and the hot glazed sand against my throat.

My Soul tasted realness in it.

Quite close to me, in immense sad beauty, were the deep high heavy silent somber hills of Montana. Today the nearer ones were a stately enchanted Blue: a Blue of all ages: a Blue of infinitude: a Blue with a feel of life and death in its Blueness. Above it the sky was not blue but a pale glimmering shimmering silver hung across with gray silk clouds soft as doves' plumage.

I sat on a flat rock and looked at all of it and at the desert around, and at my dusty shoes.

All of it felt overwhelmingly sincere: at one with the wide

worn used earth.

My dusty shoes looked to be at one with it and could interpret it.

I felt my shoes could claim their human prerogative of getting dusty in any of this world's roads.

It gave me a feeling of human Sincerity: good-and evil Safeness.

It is on me now, along with cold cream and strong memory of Desert and Sun and Blue.

It is as good as a beef-sandwich.

Better: I don't like beef-sandwich.

Frontispiece of *I, Mary MacLane* (1917)

SWIFT GO MY DAYS

Swift, Swift go my days.

By rights I think time should drag with me, for I am wasting my portion of life as I live it.

But my days pass Swift—Swift Swift.

They come, they fly away—before I know.

I'm thinking it is Tuesday: but while I'm thinking—Wednesday has come: and gone: and Thursday is rushing in. Tuesday, blue-and-gold or gray-and-silver, with its mornings and nights and bits of food and openings of doors and thinkings: Wednesday with the same equipment: Thursday the same. Each day comes and goes like a flash of filmed silvered garbled light.

But there is time in each for me to touch the enchanted Everydayness: time for the turbulent sly delight of tasting, smelling, feeling the eternal humors and romances in each small thing near me—my Clock, my Window, my Jar of Cold Cream, my Two Thumbs. There is time in each day for it to make me pay a wearing glimmering feverish homage to the mystic daily godhead.

My life exacts terrific homages from me.

I am wearing out—frailly, tiredly, from a desolate, uneasy love of living.

It is why my days go Swift when by rights time should drag leadenly in punishment for barbarous futileness.

There is not time-space enough in any of the days sufficient to love the virile green and the murderous red and the sweet pale surprising purple in the sunset above the west desert: nor space to love the smell of a sudden August rain: nor the flaming delicate Idea of the poet John Keats.

While I'm starting to love each of those to its height of love-worthiness—the today is gone: and the tomorrow, which must see a new love-game started for each Thing, is come.

But while I say 'is come': it's gone.

So Swift go my days—oh Swift, Swift!

I DON'T KNOW

The things I know are jumbled and tangled into an indescribable heap inside me.

The things I Don't Know are separated and ranged of their own volition in long orderly rows in my conscious mentality.

The things I know glow with tints and gleams and will-o'-wisp lights and primal colors and waveringly with the blinding gold-purple lightnings of all-Time. The things I Don't Know glow—each one separately—with a small precise lantern-brightness of its own. Also in my wide background are things I don't know and am unaware of it: the mass of my luminous Ignorance—it shines with an earthy phosphorescence. When I look at the things I know I get an undetailed perspective of me like a bird's-eye view of London. When I look at neat formal rows of things I Don't Know I have a clear look, as if through an uncurtained window into a bare little room, at my quietest self sitting knitting or plaiting straw.

I reckon up and count up and check up lists of big and little things I Don't Know—like this, rapidly: I Don't Know what ink is made of, nor how to fire a Maxim gun: I don't know how to make a will: I don't know how to cook a prairie-chicken, nor what to feed a pet weasel, nor who invented the snarling-iron, nor what it is.

I Don't Know what food people eat in the Himalaya Mountains, nor how Lord Cornwallis felt when he surrendered: I don't know the color of a chicken's gizzard, nor of sand, nor of fish-scales, nor of mice: I don't know whether an English cabinet minister needs strength of mind or strength of will, or both, or neither.

I Don't Know how I hurt the true heart of my friend: I don't know astronomy nor solid geometry: I don't know what I think with: I don't know what ooze leather is, nor who pitched for the Tigers in nineteen-nine.

I Don't Know a good horse from a bad horse: I don't know why a bat sleeps head downward, nor what wasps live on: I don't know how to open oysters, nor how to milk a cow: I don't know the Latin for 'whiskey.'

I Don't Know whether friendship is a selfish or an unselfish thing, nor who discovered the medlar apple: I don't know what is a jab, fistically speaking, nor a punch, nor a hook, nor a wallop, nor the fighting weight of Packey McFarland: I don't know whether a moth 'marries' or whether her eggs are impregnated like a fish's: I don't know why a clasp knife is called a jack knife, nor what to do for an aching foot.

I Don't Know how glass is blown: I don't know whether coal is vegetable or mineral: I don't know the chemical composition of the sunset vapors, nor how to play euchre: I don't know how many guns an armored cruiser carries, nor whether a gorilla meditates—I don't know whether I hate or greatly admire Catherine and Marie de Medici: I don't know a winch from a windlass.

I Don't Know where is the cinnamon bear's native haunt: I don't know how flint is mined, nor if wire is made of steel: I don't know who was the better man—William Wordsworth or the Duke of Wellington: I don't know the advantages of tariff revision downward: I don't know where ex-President Taft will go when he dies.

I Don't Know whether I feel more comfortable with or without my stays: I don't know the origin of the word 'dogged': I don't know whether a 'full house' is better than 'two pairs,' nor whether a right merry heart today is better than a wrong contented mind to-morrow: I don't know whether rabbit-pie is made of cats in Paris, nor how many sails has a sloop: I don't know what makes a dead body rot.

I Don't Know how to sharpen a carving knife, nor how to roll a cigarette: I don't know the real English meaning of the French noun 'élancement': I don't know whether my sex is a matter of my genital organs or of my mental inwards: I don't know how to determine the contents of a circle in square inches, nor how to pronounce 'zebra.'

I Don't Know whether Edgar Allan Poe is big or little: I don't know how many soldiers fell at Shiloh: I don't know whether temperament or nature or circumstance makes one woman a happy kindhearted whore and another an unhappy cruel-hearted nun: I don't know how to grow artichokes: I don't know what brimstone is, nor how to play the accordion: I don't know what quality in me forms my handwriting.

I Don't Know what-like was my Soul in the Stone Age: I don't know whether cheese is good or bad for my health: I don't know what becomes of discarded hairpins, nor a tooth-brush's ultimate destiny: I don't know the 'Fra Diavolo' opera, nor whether anyone ever uses the word 'thwack.'

I Don't Know whether my heart breaks from within or without: I don't know whether 'good old Marie Lloyd' of the London 'halls' has a brain like G. K. Chesterton or a dexterous individuality like a juggler: I don't know whether I feel spiritual bliss in my knees or in my spirit: I don't know why I breathe and go on breathing.

I Don't Know what became of the ten lost tribes of Israel: I don't know how to say how-do-you-do to a king: I don't know the exact meaning of my terror and despair: I don't know why I love—why I ever love—

I Don't Know whether laws of chance govern a spinning roulette wheel and ivory ball or whether chance is beyond law: I don't know what kind of missile a Krupp gun shoots: I don't know how a ground-and-lofty tumbler turns a triple air-summersault: I don't know whether I really am the way I look in the mirror: I don't know whether the Russian language has Romanic roots: I don't know what is the wild power in poetry.

I Don't Know whether lust is a human coarseness or a human fineness: I don't know why death holds a so sweet lure since it would take away my Body: I don't know that I wouldn't deny my Christ, if I had one, three times before a given cockcrow: I don't know on the other hand that I would: I don't know whether honor is a reality in human beings or a pose: I don't know that I mayn't be able to think with my Body when it is in its coffin.

I Don't Know what makes each day a Day of dark Gold and life mournfully precious: I don't know where is God: I don't know how they make tea in Ireland: I don't know how to pronounce the word 'girl': I don't know how to make lace: I don't know whether I hear a sound or feel it, nor why a spool of thread looks exactly like a Spool of Thread. I Don't Know—I Don't Know—I Don't Know, rapidly, to the end of the mystic common-place infinitudes.

—those give me a clear look, as if through an uncurtained window into a bare little room, at my quietest self sitting knitting or plaiting straw—

Originally titled "Knitting or Plaiting Straw"

COLD BOILED POTATO

It's a Sunday midnight and I've just eaten a Cold Boiled Potato.

I shall never be able to write one-tenth of my fondness for a Cold Boiled Potato.

A Cold Boiled Potato is always an unpremeditated episode which is its chief charm.

It's nice to happen on a book of poetry on a windowsill. It's nice to surprise a square of chocolate in a glove box. It's nice to come upon a little yellow apple in ambush. It's nice to get an unexpected letter from Jane Gillmore. It's nice to unearth a reserve fund of silk stockings under a sofa pillow. And especially it's nice to find a Cold Boiled Potato on a pantry shelf at midnight.

I like caviar at luncheon. And I like venison at dinner, dark and bloody and rich. And I like champagne bubbling passionately in a hollow-stemmed glass on New Year's day. And I like terrapin turtle. And I like French-Canadian game-pie. And artichokes and grapes and baby onions. And none of them has the odd gnome-ish charm of a Cold Boiled Potato at midnight.

I can imagine no circumstance in which a Cold Boiled Potato would not take precedent with me at midnight. If I had a broken arm: if I had a husband lying dead in the next room: if I were facing abrupt worldly disaster: if there were a burglar in the house: if I'd had a dayful of depression: if God and opportunity were knocking and clamoring at my door: I should disregard each and all some minutes at midnight if I had also a Cold Boiled Potato.

I love to read Keats's *Nightingale* in my hushed life. I love to remember Caruso at the Metropolitan singing *Celeste Aida*. I love to watch the bewitching blonde Blanche Sweet in a moving picture. I love to feel the summer moonlight on my eyelids. And it's disarmingly contented I am with a Cold Boiled Potato at midnight.

Content is my rarest emotion and I get it at midnight out of a Cold Boiled Potato.

Some things in life thrill me. Some drive me garbledly mad. Some uplift me. Some debauch me. Some strengthen and enlighten me. Some hurt, hurt, hurt. But I'm not thrilled nor maddened nor uplifted nor debauched nor strengthened nor enlightened nor hurt, but only fed-up and fattened in spirit by a Cold Boiled Potato at midnight.

I stand in the pantry door leaning against the jamb, with a tiny glass salt-shaker in one hand and the sweet dark pink Cold Boiled Potato in the other, And I sprinkle it with salt and I nibble, nibble, nibble. And I say aloud, 'Gee, it's good!'

I liked Cold Boiled Potato at four-and twenty. I liked it at seventeen. I liked it at twelve. At three I climbed on cake-boxes in search of one. And now in the deep bloom of being myself I am made roundly replete at midnight with a Cold Boiled Potato.

A Cold Boiled Potato—it tastes of chestnuts at midnight, the first frost-kissed chestnuts in the woods: and it tastes of rain-water and of salt and of roses: it tastes of young willow-bark and of earth and of grass-stems: it tastes of the sun and the wind and of some nameless relishingness born of the summer hillside that grew it: it tastes at midnight so *like* a Cold Boiled Potato.

A precious peach-colored orchid, an antique spiderweb-like lace handkerchief, a delicate purple butterfly, an emerald bracelet: I'd strive for each of those in an eagerly casual way. But it's like an ogre at midnight I pounce on a Cold Boiled Potato.

A Cold Boiled Potato reminds me of the Dickens books in which so much food is eaten cold and tastes so savory—even the 'wilderness of cold potatoes' portioned to the Marchioness by Sally Brass. And it reminds me of the Rip Van Winkle play—'give this fellow a cold potato and let him go.' And it reminds me of Hamlet—funeral baked meats might include it. And it reminds me of Robin Hood's merry men, and Huckleberry Finn, and the Canterbury Pilgrims, and the Prodigal Son, and all the picturesque wayfarers. It reminds me of the poor as a colorful race wrapped around with hungry romance. It reminds me that life is full of life—rich and fruitful and evolutionary and cosmic: few things feel so cosmic as a Cold Boiled Potato at midnight. It makes me want as I nibble to plant a field of potatoes on a southern-exposed hill and hoe them and dig them all by myself: and give all but one to the poor and Boil that to eat Cold at midnight.

I have to be very hungry to crave a Cold Boiled Potato, but being hungry no possible morsel of food can so interest me at midnight. The same potato hot is domestic and tasteless. The same potato at ten in the evening lukewarm within and sodden with memories of dinner, is a repellent item. At midnight it is all unexpected magnetism. At midnight my whole being is profoundly courteous, wooingly cordial toward a Cold Boiled Potato.

If I had only what I deserved my portion might well be a Cold Boiled Potato. Intrinsically it is rated low and I know me to be a sort of jezebel. But I'd wonder each midnight if whoever metes out the deserts in this surprising universe knew with what gust I rise at it—*would* I get it.

Nor am I satisfied like the meek and lowly with my midnight supper of Cold Boiled Potato: damn the meek and lowly. It's a satanic delight I take in it. It's a sly private orgie I make of it: a pirate's banquet, a thieves' picnic, a pagan rite, a heathen revelry, a conceit all and unhallowedly my own. My thoughts as I nibble are set mostly on my villainies. No food I eat brings me so broad a license of feeling—a sense of freedom—as a Cold Boiled Potato at midnight.

On a Cold Boiled Potato at midnight I am lightly valorous: call me a trickster and I'll call you a rotter: call me a liar and I'll call you a traitor: call me a coward and I'll call you another: not pugnaciously but gayly and serenely.

I am then in my most bespeaking mood. Anyone who met me standing nibbling in a pantry doorway at midnight would be charmed. I would talk with a dainty ribaldry and offer to share the feast.

For shadow-things piled too near God compensates me in unexpected midnights with a Cold Boiled Potato: along with it a pantry doorway to stand in and a little glass salt-shaker to hold in my other hand.

Original title: "God Compensates Me"

THE BACK OF A MAGAZINE

All my life I've liked the Back of a magazine.

Some black-browed Wednesday I purchase a magazine, a fifteen-cent one, and read it through. I read the stories and they deeply engage or lightly interest me. I read the 'special articles' and if they tell about flying machines or wild birds or hospitals or woman-prisoners in penitentiaries they charm or absorb my thoughts. I look at the illustrations and try to decide whether they are art or science or mechanism. I read the verse and if it's poetry it exhilarates me as if closed shutters were opened to let Day into a gloomy Room. Then I read the advertisements in the Back and they do all of those things to me in comforting lifegiving oxygen-furnishing ways. Each advertisement is a short story with an eerie little 'plot' in it: each is a special article full of purpose: each is fruitful poetry: and in my two hands I all but have and hold those wonderful Things they exploit.

They make me feel it's my birthday and I'm presented a wealth of lavish gifts.

They make me feel it's all a world of playthings.

They make me feel like a baby with a rattle, a ball and a hoop of bells.

I like *everything* in the Back of a magazine.

I like the Revolvers, handsome plausible shortbarreled Revolvers with pictures of ordinary people in dim-lit midnight bedrooms, and ordinary expected-looking burglars climbing in windows—Revolvers of ten shots and of six, and of different calibers, and all of them gleamingly mystically desirable: I like the Soaps, smooth amorous appetizing Soaps, some in luxurious Paris packets, and others spread out in blue water and rosy foam, splashed in by athletic Archimedesque young men and fat creamy babies and slim beautiful ladies—Mary Garden Soap of pungent delicious scent, tar Soap for the long lovely hair of girls, austere Ivory Soap it floats: I like the Rubber Heels of resilient charm so tellingly pictured and described that at once I desire them beneath my spirit-heels—springy and solid and thick and firm: I like the Tooth-pastes and Tooth-powders and Tooth-lotions in tubes and tins and bottles, each bearing beneficent messages to the human white teeth of this world—one unfailing kind coming lyrically out like a ribbon and lying flat on the brush: I like the foods—of miraculous spotless purity and enticement—Biscuits and Chocolate and Figs, and *Foie-gras* in thick glossy little pots, so richly pictured and sung that merely to let my thoughts graze in their pasturage fattens my Heart: I like the men's very thin Watches, and men's Garters—no metal can touch you—, and men's fluffy-lathered shaving sticks, and men's trim smart flawless tailored Suits, in none of which I have use or interest until I find them in the Back of a magazine—where at once they grow charming and romantic: I like the jars and boxes and tubes and glasses of Cold Cream, Cold Cream fit for skins of goddesses, fit for elves to feed on—a soft satiny scented snow-white elysium of wax and vaseline and almond paste, pictured in forty alluring shapes till it feels pleasantly ecstatic just to be living in the same world with bewitching vases of Cold Cream, Cold Cream, Cold Cream—always bewitching and lovely but never so notably and festively as in the Back of a magazine: and I like the Pencils: and Book-cases: and Silver: and Jewels: and Glass: and cloves: and Shoes—beautiful Shoes: and Fountain-pens: and Leather things: and Paint—silkish salubrious Paints, house-Paints, and the panegyrics with them—they make me long to own a spirit-house and paint it liberally: and Rugs: and Varnish: and Clothes—wonderful Clothes: and Bungalows: and Phonographs—his master's voice: and Paper—fine-wrought Paper to write on—bond and linen and hand-pressed, pale-tinted—a vast virgin treasure: and Oranges: and Cigarettes—a shilling in London a quarter here: and Water—Bottles of powdery rubber: and Stockings—patrician Stockings which take me into realms of silk-looms and delicate dyes and slim ankles: and Candle-Shades: and Candle-Sticks: and countless Cosmetics—Cosmetics of tender colors for the outer woman: and Sealingwax indescribably useless and attractive: and Tennis-Racquets: and Ivory—smooth Vantine Ivory toys and trinkets polished softly bright as moonlight—and their lily-worded descriptions like restrained sonnets: and Washing Powders—let the Gold Dust twins do your work: and Shower-baths: and Evans' Ale: and Flying Boats: and Umbrellas: and Cameras—if it isn't an Eastman it isn't a kodak: and boxes of Candy—sweet wilderness of chocolates—their very makers' names have a melting gust—Allegretti, Huyler, Clarence Crane, Maillard—cloying courtiers all: and Diamond Dyes—a child can use them: and Veranda Screens—she can look out but he can't look in: and Cedar Chests: and Chartreuse from Carthusian monasteries: and Perfumes—Perfumes in their maddening-sweet pride, Perfumes from Paris, Perfumes bottled in thick crystal, enchantingly costly—each American dollar added to their price-by-the-ounce making them fragranter to my thoughts: and boxes of benevolent Matches, and captivating Brooms, and fascinating Scouring-powders—a Dutch girl on the can chasing dirt—all three luscious tempting things in the Back of a magazine: and Automobiles—ask the man who owns one: and Rifles—simple and formidable and fine: and restful Rat-poison—they die in the open air seeking water: and sacks of Flour—eventually why not now—flour unusual and piquant in the Back of a magazine, flour novel and endearing: and Type-writers: and Mushrooms: and MonkeyWrenches: and Rosaries: and Rock-salt—

the Back, the Back, the Back of a magazine—

There's no sadness and no terror in the Back of a magazine.

And it is for Everybody, Everybody.

A million people read a story in the middle of the magazine and half the million readily miss its point. But a single tin of Talcum Powder in the Back—the whole million note that and miss nothing in it: it gets to them both on and under their skin.

Some of the million read a ten-line poem in *vers libre* in the front of the magazine—and nine-tenths of their number are hard-put to it: the mentalities of this human race being mostly shops shut down. It is something pregnant and prophetic to a poet, merely musical to a plain prose writer, arrant folly to a telephone girl, amusing nonsense to a butcher, a comic fantasy to a milliner, a form of insanity to a plumber, an unknown tongue to a milk-man, a kind of sin to a Baptist minister. But to each of those a Can of Soup in the Back of the same magazine has easily, exactly the same ox-tail-ish meanings: it reaches them where they live.

A thousand persons agree with an article about atavism in orang-outangs and ten thousand more quite refute it. But they all harmoniously commit suicide with the same make of Revolver—hammer the hammer—or get rousing drunk to the same degree with the same brand of high-powered whiskey—Wilson, that's all.

A countess, a courtesan and a convict-woman summarily pass over the front and middle of the magazine as containing nothing to their purpose. But like jungle denizens at their drinking pool the three of them meet hostilely on the common ground of a popular Cigarette featured in the Back—a blend to suit every taste—wherewith they unwittingly smoke away half their generic differentiations. The Colonel's Lady and Judy o'Grady anoint themselves nightly into a state of shining invisible kinship from separated twin jars of the same bewitching Cold Cream.

I'm not sure myself and Miss Lily Walker of the Broadway chorus regard similarly a beauteous box of Rice Powder: she perchance would at once dash madly into it and powder herself o'er with it, whereas I would fain ponder about it awhile as a tiny bevioleted adventure. But pondering or powdering, equally exciting to each of us is its delicate pale lilac blazonment in the Back of a magazine.

The front of the magazine may mean little to you and the middle of the magazine may mean nothing to me: the Back of it none of us escapes.

It is for Everybody, Everybody.

Even Senegambians: they can look at the pictures and marvel over them.

I can there meet a Senegambian on the common ground of it might be a delicate transparent oval of Pears' Soap, pretty as a jewel of price: perchance we would each unconsciously feel we wouldn't be happy till we got it.

It's only as playthings I want the Things in the Back of a magazine.

To me they are toys, lyrics of matter, food of the senses.

The octroi would have no sympathy with my loiterings among their wares. It is a fête of my own, indolent and fanciful, unrecognized in commerce. Any article I may put to its forthright use in actuality becomes an idyllic toy when I find it in the Back of a magazine. The desirable Revolvers are not firearms with which to shoot myself and burglars, but only bijous to have and handle and caress. The luxuriant vervain- and violet-scented Soaps are not for my toilet, but something to eat, for my astral body to feed on—nourishing food they make. The lush Cold Creams have no massaging possibilities in them—they are for my thoughts to gambol among, for my meddlesome spirit-fingers to touch and fuss with deliciously, blissfully, transcending all vulgar use. The men's thin Watches mean nothing to me as Watches: and their Garters—what's it to me whether no-metal-can-touch-you or no-metal-at-all? My thoughts merely revel and juggle with them, picture and legend—they are pastimes of my child-self. The cream-woven Note Papers are not to write on but wherewithal to imagine how cool and smooth they would feel drawn slowly across my flushed cheek. A sack of Flour—I feel only how I'd like to have it spilled out—eventually—why-not-now—in a thick warm-tinted heap on the blue-velvety floor of my room that I might roll and bathe in it and feel it feathery-fluffy on my skin.

So I play with my toys on black-browed Wednesdays. Some Wednesdays even fail to be black-browed because there are Backs to magazines.

Original title: "Black-browed Wednesdays"

TO WANDER AND BANG AND FLOAT ABOUT

My damnedest damningest quality is Wavering—Wavering—

I might say I prefer the dawn to the twilight or the twilight to the dawn.

Neither would be true.

I love the dawn—I love the twilight.

What I unconsciously *prefer* is the long negative Wavering space-of-day between the two.

I might say I prefer heaven to hell or hell to heaven. Neither would be true.

My garbled gyral nature, partaking uneasily of both, prefers to wander and hang and float about between the two.

I might say I prefer strength to weakness or weakness to strength.

Neither would be true.

What I prefer is a hellish hovering, an endless torturing Tenterhook between the two.

And that Wavering preference is against my will, against my reason, against my judgment, against my taste and liking—against my life, my welfare, my salvation: against the clear lights of my spirit. I know I work intently and industriously at the articles of my damnation in the Wavering—Wavering—

I know it would be better to die at once: failing that, to live but to live positively as a beggar, a whore, a thief or a milliner. Knowing that, I know also I Waver: I know I shall prefer to Waver: I know I shall constantly Waver.

I am constant—I am remarkably profoundly constant—in my Wavering.

In the morning as I dress I draw on a stocking—a long black or white glistening stocking. I know I do it only because the mixed big world, which refuses to Waver, is pushing—pushing me. I would choose if I could—though loathing my choice—to stay with my bare foot and my stocking in my hand, Wavering. Between drawing it on and pausing barefoot, Wavering. I prefer not to draw on the stocking: I prefer not to be barefoot: I prefer Wavering—Wavering—

When I'm hungry I choose: not to let food alone: not to eat it: to have it by me and Waver, Waver emptily. Not to enjoy its anticipation: not to contemplate it. No—*no*! To *Waver*! I reach and take the food because the world in its pushing pushes me.

If the world stopped pushing—

One reason it will be pleasant to be dead: I can then no longer Waver.

Worms will eat me unwaveringly. Or they may then do the Wavering. But *I* shall no more pause with a bare foot and an empty stocking, a dish of food and a gnawing midriff.

Here I sit as yet, alive and Wavering.

The Wavering is not the pale cast of thought: it is not my way of analysis: it is only Wavering—Wavering—

Wavering is not among the blue-green Stones in my antique necklace: not by that name—not as one Stone.

It is a marked and hateful and hellish gift of this present Me who house my Soul.

It is half of this Mary MacLane—who is I—: and I know.

I am constant alone—noticeably tensely constant—in my Wavering: and less constant in Wavering than in the ghoulish preference.

An odd and subtle doom.

DEVIL

An old rascal mentioned in the Bible, now reported engaged to Mary McLane.

From *The Foolish Dictionary* (1904)

A THOUSAND KISSES

Among my other gifts I own also Wantonness. In proof of which I am wishing as I sit here for a Thousand careless kisses: eleven o'clock of stiff evening—a Thousand Kisses. A wonderful, wonderful attribute, Wantonness: rich, rich luster in the conscious temperament which owns it, a Gift-thing delicate and gorgeous.

By it I want a Thousand Kisses: a Thousand—made all of Wantonness.

Kisses come in differing kinds and only one is Wanton.

The kiss of a lover has an intense cosmic use: the kiss of a mother is tender fostering food: the kiss of a friend is vantage and grace of friendliness: the kiss of a child is cool charm of snowflakes and green springtime leaves.

And the kiss of Wantonness is not of use, nor of food, nor of gracing vantage, nor of childhood charm—but is restless essence of humanness and worldliness and mere sheer limitless encompassing liking: born of sweet lips, alien it might be, and secretly 'unattuned,' but warm and fond and present: answering the pathos of infinite jejuneness which flows, flows always in red human blood.

Through the race rides a long dread wistfulness, made of tears and lies and the barbaric distress and pitfall of everyday's journey: a crying wish for a cup of warmed drugged sweet ease to turn it all a moment away: but a moment away.

And through all the race is the measureless poetry, purling and mantling in its bowl of flesh. Each human one is made of the sun, and made of the moon, and made of the four winds and the seas and the last pink sea-foam on the crests of the twilit waves: and made of salt and of sugar and of lonesome calling of loons and quick song of skylarks: and made of sword-edges and of money and of dolls and toys and painted glass: and made of loose reckless shuffling of dry autumn leaves, and of nerves and of illusions and of broken food and hesitance: and made of Mother-Goose rhymes and of cigarette ashes and of raveled silk: and made of layers and layers of mixed-up passionate colors and of gilded cakes and of strawberries and of temperamental orgasms and raw slivery onions and gaming and dancing and minute-by-minute inconsistency: all veiled in a thin gold veil—all in a thin gold veil. Betwixt the wistfulness and the poetry—*hélas*, what chance has the human equation, unsought, unwarned, unchallenged of God to be straitly equable!

No chance.

Happily no chance.

Thus I, Mary MacLane, so conscious of Me and garbledly gifted, want a Thousand Kisses at eleven o'clock of a still evening.

No spirit-hands of Love are laid soft on my drooping shoulders in the passing days: no Love—no Love in all my life.

No miracle Wonder and Gentleness stirs in and against my Heart: my Heart is strangely dead of a strange Realness, known and felt but unachieved:—no Love—no Love in my life.

And I can wish for no Love, for the listless Heart is listlessly dead.

I wish instead, in hastening present clock-ticking moments, for a Thousand present-warmed Kisses: a thousand in Wanton response to a Wanton 'leven-o'clock.

Dominating waving washing warmth of Wantonness, compassing me at eleven o'clock.

A Thousand careless insouciant Kisses: a Thousand gorgeous delicate Kisses: a round Thousand. From what lips—whose lips—what do I know?—: so their Kisses are a Thousand.

From what lips—what do I care?—: so they be eager and live and tenderly false.

—come some of the Thousand glowing on my pink lips, and my white fingers, which were tense, relax

—come more of the Thousand, and my rigid hard-riding thoughts grow drowsy and pliant and negligible.

—come more of the Thousand, and my knees and the marrow in my bones are gently aware of most logical opiate ease—

—come more of the Thousand, and my midriff is full of cream-and-chocolate casualness and my smooth arms are washed down with mists of custom.

—come more of the Thousand, and my seven senses start to melt at the edges

—come more of the Thousand, and the palms of my hands wax merely pleasant-feeling and the soles of my feet fatly comfortable—

—come the last of the Thousand in a swirling silly lovely lightly-insane shower—and I feel exactly like a woman in the next street who goes forth clad in mustard-and-cerise with a devilish black-and-white Valeska-Suratt parasol: and more—much more—I feel the way she *looks*—

For this Wanton-thing is not amour but psychology: in it I am less the maenad than the philosopher: less the Cyprian woman than the Muse.

I am a deeply gifted woman.

I am not prone on my green couch, frayed, frazzled, bowed-down in spirit from a day of frightful stress and cross-purpose.

Instead, hair-triggerishly alive, with definite desire beating hotly this moment in my throat: the wish for Kisses—Kisses far removed from Death and Graves and Coffins: Kisses of this present clock-tickingness, Kisses useless, meaningless, sweet—oh, sweet!—

—in number, a Thousand: in kind, Wanton.

A RIGHT SHAPE AND SIZE

Sometimes I fancy me married—a responsible wife, a housekeeping matron: with my window-sills full of potted plants. I have a woman quality which seems uxoresque: I am someway a Right Shape and Size to be somebody's wife. My bodily and astral dimensions have outlines apparently suitable for something in the married-woman way.

The wild piquance of being myself—who but for extreme saneness would be mad—rises up and smashes that concept.

But being a Right Shape and Size I involuntarily imagine it.

Fleetingly I imagine a flat in the West Seventies in New York, or a bungalow on the Jersey side, or a middle-sized house in a middle-sized town in Middle West Illinois—whichever might happen—with me set marriedly down in the midst of it like a suitable maggot in a suitable nut. Suitableness, diametrically opposed to Romance, is its keynote.

I fancy me walking about my married house mornings after breakfast in a neat linen dress and high-heeled satin slippers: snipping dead leaves off my windowsill plants, dusting bits of porcelain, giving my maid some tame household directions. My Body looks slender and supple and newly-married and in-the-drawing in the linen house-dress. The geometric gods regard me with immense satisfaction as being an exact proved theorem. I go to the telephone to order some Little Neck clams and some vermouth cocktails for dinner, and a roast and some Brussels sprouts and the assemblings of a salad: and in it I am ingrainedly domestic, dreadfully useful, a strong pillar of the vast good nice world. Afternoons I go out to a modiste's to fit a gown, or to a mild bridge-party along with other suitable women, or to a matinée with a suitable neighbor. Everything is perfectly right in my insides and in my thoughts: my thoughts run in little troughs in which there is no leakage or deviation, thoughts of a dreadful niceness, thoughts which ever presuppose potted plants on my window-sills.

Evenings I go out with my husband, or sit around with my husband, or take leave of him. for a few hours at the hall door. My husband would be the sort of man that is called a Good Scout. And he would have married me not for my wistfulness or wickedness or weirdness but for that I am a proper Shape and Size, with a smooth proper covering of flesh, to make a suitable sizable wife. And he would be a heavy grappling anchor to hold me fast in an ocean of domesticness.

Men of the genus Good Scout are all fiercely alike.

All women, no matter what their genus, are exceptions to the rule. But men—rich men, poor men, beggar-men, thieves: so only they are Good Scouts—are of marvelous sameness. It comes from the want of minute lifelong pinpricking care of petticoats and potted plants—a detailed intensely personal sort of pain which touches dull solid tones of individuality with vivid various spots of color.

Men are made in 'job lots' like their own cravats. Their cravats will differ in texture and color and quality and price. But each one is innately necktie. Use it as a garter or a tourniquet or a strangler's noose: it still is a man's deadly necktie. Its use may be ruined but its necktique is deathless. Except poets—and perhaps scientists—men are themselves like that. They cannot get away from the Adam. Nor can women get away from the Eve. But Eve was not a type but a somewhat pleasant human ensemble. While Adam was a type and a sufficiently nasty one: a rotter and a welcher: doubtless the Good Scout type of his day.

A Good Scout is the sort of man who if a woman trusts him with one one-hundredth of her heart will take the whole heart and twist and batter it: and read the paper and smoke his pipe and pay the bills: serenely unaware.

Which is beside the point in this. For in this image all my marriedness is a thing of outer Shape and Size and Suitableness. The odd but natural sequence is that I make an excellent wife. Excellent is the word. I keep a neat house with no dust left in the corners and no dead leaves on the potted plants. My husband is well looked after as to breakfasts and dinners and bodily comfort, and I am rigidly square with him and chastely true to him.

If, some dinnertime, as I sit opposite him in a soft pretty chiffon gown, my secret thoughts overflow their troughs and I passionately forget the potted plants and the window-sills and want horribly to rise up and bloodily murder my husband for being such a Good Scout: that would be a genuinely powerless matter, a cobweb, trifle, compared with my actual potent Shape and Size which are so suitable for a wife.

I make truly and simply an excellent wife.

—by God and my Soul-and-bones! it would be honester, finer, sweeter—more *comfortable* to be the dirty beggar-woman in the wet slippery streets—

But it's facilely fancied because I am of Right Dimensions to be some Good Scout's wife.

A curious subtly pitfalled world: in it my Shape and Size, and my Weight which is also Right, could betray me into being an excellent wife: and by that a lying chattel, an inexpressibly damaged woman.

MY FRIEND
ANNABEL LEE

BY

Mary MacLane

Chicago
Herbert S. Stone and Company
MCMIII

The original title-page, 1903 (reduced)

Selected Articles

AT CONEY ISLAND

Well, and by this time, having been in the mysterious East days and weeks, I have gazed at several things as you may imagine. I have not come into the mysterious East to learn and live, but rather to gaze and inquire. And so I gaze and inquire, and gaze and inquire, sometimes perfunctorily, sometimes quite desperately, sometimes very heavily. But always with dogged persistence and the fresh candor of youth. (I don't know what the fresh candor of youth is, but I like the look of it—when written.) And in so doing I have come upon some rather good things—some very good things, in fact.

By far the best thing yet is Coney Island.

One bright, pretty day I—of Butte, Montana—in company with a Little Chaperone-person went out to Coney Island to gaze and inquire. Coney Island leaves nothing to be desired. Everything is there. God is in his heaven and all's right with the world. It is delicious.

The first thing one gazes at is the beach and the humanity thereupon—especially the children. Little Billy and little Alice and little Katie and little Henry dig and splash and shovel and kick and burrow in the sand. And their legs are bare—it is here indeed that one realizes the glory of bare legs.

"They have no stockings and shoes," I said to the Little Chaperone-person, wistfully.

"They have not," murmured the Little Chaperone-person, with a note of envy in her voice.

"They have knees—knees of their own. My dear, do you realize that they have knees of their own?" I exclaimed.

The Little Chaperone-person nodded.

And we thought straightway of the time when we had also been six—and had knees—the Little Chaperone-person and I.

There were all kinds of children on the beach at Coney Island. I thought that I had seen in Butte, Montana all the kinds of children that the world contains. But no. Here upon the beach at Coney Island I found worlds unknown. There was a little girl lying buried in the sand—only a touzled head, a tanned flat little face, and two hard brown fists were visible. I felt a distinct pleasure in gazing at this. There seemed something fine and desirable about the figure of a tiny girl in the sand.

"Look," I said to the Little Chaperone-person.

"Yes," she made answer. The Little Chaperone-person is an extremely appreciative one.

We walked over to the child.

"Do you like the sand, little girl?" I asked.

"Yes, ma'm," replied the child. The child's eyes were the common but lovely eyes of a real child. She looked out of them as always a child looks.

"Why do you like it?" I went on.

"'Cause it's sand," she replied.

"What is your name?" I ventured.

"Gertrude," replied the child. The wind and water were mixed in Gertrude's hair. Gertrude's little life was full of weather. "I am six," she added hastily to forestall any questions upon that point.

"Does it feel good to be six?" I inquired.

"I dunno," said Gertrude.

"You are extremely fortunate in not knowing," I observed. "It's hell—just hell—to know, sometimes."

"Huh!" said Gertrude, with wide startled eyes.

"Yes, it is," I repeated, "but never mind. Good-by."

"Good-by," replied the child. She sat up in the sand and stared, stared, stared, as always a child stares.

Dear little Gertrude—

"Isn't it very well," I said, "to be six, and not to know it?"

"Oh, very well," assented the Little Chaperone-person.

"And look at this beach," I added, "and all the people on it who are only six."

"They will always be six," said the Little Chaperone-person.

Just then there came a heavy masculine individual of the whiskey-drinking kind and interrupted us. "Lady-could-you-give-me-a-few-cents-for-the-love-of-God-I'm-dead-broke-and"—We gave him the few cents—not for the love of God, however. Rather because we wished him to go and get drunk.

He was already half-seas over.

"That was not six, certainly," said the Little Chaperone-person.

"No, I think that was about five," I replied, with my most positive intonation.

And also upon the beach we came upon a stout old lady who was sitting upright while another packed sand about her in a damp heavy bank. These were not wearing bathing suits, but were in ordinary clothes. The stout old lady sat stiff for this process as she would have sat for a shoe polish or a shampoo.

Often as I've gazed and inquired in my life I have never before beheld anything quite like this.

"What would you call that?" I asked the Little Chaperone-person.

"That is a bit of scenic effect," she replied, meaninglessly.

"Doubtless," I rejoined with equal idiocy.

We both enjoyed the moment thoroughly.

The entire beach was picturesquely infested with humanity.

A man and a girl in their scant flannel garments were sitting side by side in the sand. They ogled. They coquetted. They languished. They were two lovers. We agreed—the Little Chaperone-person and I—that it did not require a brilliant intellect to divine that.

"Don't speak to them," said the Little Chaperone-person. Much as I wished to gaze and inquire, we avoided them as if they had been a grievous plague.

And a lone girl sat with her back to the sounding sea. "What on earth," I began. "Don't ask me," said the Little Chaperone-person. "Let it go—it's perfect as it is. Which was true enough.

And the most delicate little incongruity of all was the very slim figure of young lad stretched out on the sand reading—would you believe it—*Villette*, by Charlotte Brontë. "Did you suppose," I said to to the Little Chaperone-person, "that anyone ever read that now—particularly a boy!"

"I am not thinking of that so much," she made answer, "as of that bookplate on this beach, Coney Island, New York."

After which we walked on in ruminating silence.

Then we went to gaze at that steeplechase arrangement. There are some things at Coney Island that are altogether delightful, but there are two things at least that are simple monstrosities. So much so indeed that it gives one thrills and spasms of pleasure to gaze at them and to talk about them. The steeplechase arrangement is one of them. The grown persons who went in for that were very young. Their shoulders moved and their necks curved exactly as if they were six years old, and the short detached sentences that came from their lips were very well done. "Happy childhood," we said.

And the other monstrosity is the loop-the-loop affair. To merely gaze at this gives one a decided sensation. To make the brief, frantic little journey one must be like a thing that never was on land or sea. The Little Chaperone-person and I stared in rapture at a young woman who had either misjudged her powers, or else had been told that the proper thing to do was to yell. She yelled. Her mouth opened and emitted loud whoops at irregular intervals on the frantic journey. Her facial expression was a marvel, a caution, a symphony.

"Now, what do you think of," I inquired, "when you see a thing like that?"

"Oh," mused the Little Chaperone-person, "I think of a pink parasol and a little green bottle of cucumber pickles. What do you think of?"

"Of the world, the flesh, and the devil," I replied instantly with another of my most positive intonations.

For a moment we enjoyed life.

Then we came upon a succession of interesting and heterogeneous things.

There was a box that was labeled "Drop in a cent and see twelve—astounding pictures of the war in South Africa—twelve." We dropped in a cent. The pictures were very astounding—the most astounding I have ever seen. And what I liked was the expression of the Little Chaperone-person's face as she looked at them—the delicate incongruity of them. And we came to another box labeled "Drop in a cent and hear twelve—popular songs—twelve." We dropped in a cent. The songs were extremely popular—and it was evident that the entire twelve were given out at one and the same time.

"Lovely," said the Little Chaperone-person and I.

And we came to a building where one might eat things if

one's stomach were strong and one's digestion good. We watched a man consume an egg, and then we turned hastily and walked away. And we came to a barnlike structure labeled "The Johnstown Flood." We ventured inside and looked at it. "There is almost too much striking stage-effect," I remarked. "And almost too many foamy billows," added the Little Chaperone-person.

Then we peered into a room where all the machinery in Coney Island was plainly situated. It smelled of steam and grease. And in the midst of pipes and boilers a hand-made peacock with a glass tail was perched. He was a delicate little incongruity. "That glass tail," we said as with one voice. It alone was well worth the price of admission.

And we came to a dry-goods box where a man with a soiled but angelic countenance expressed a great willingness to make tin-type photographs of you providing you gave him two dimes in advance. I gave him two dimes in advance and he made two tin-type photographs. I suppose they were of me. At any rate I had no reliable information to the contrary. I looked healthy in those pictures. A young person of feminine persuasion brought them to us hot from the camera. The Little Chaperone-person accidentally drew her tiny thumb across one of them, leaving a mark. "Now look what you did!" said the young person in a tense, strained, heavy voice. The Little Chaperone-person recoiled with a sudden serpentine movement. "Oh, let's get out of here," she whispered. We got out.

Then we came to a platform scale that was labeled "Your weight and your fortune told for one cent." This was an opportunity that we could not afford to lose. The Little Chaperone-person weighed one hundred and three pounds and I weighed one hundred and seven. Our fortunes were the same. The four pounds difference in weight made no difference, it seemed. Our fortune was: "The person you love is waiting for you in advance. Don't fail to have courage." "Isn't it a most astonishing thing that the person we love is waiting for us in advance?" I said, wonderingly. She agreed absolutely.

Even out in Butte, Montana I had never heard of anything to equal that. It seemed to require a great deal of gazing and inquiring.

By this time the shades of night had made tracks over the beach, and the Little Chaperone-person and I wandered into the Bowery. My recollection of the Bowery takes the form of a hall where you must drink beer and gaze at a brilliantly-colored semi-circle of persons with legs who sit around on a stage and sing, one after another, desperately, frantically, loudly and with amazing voices. These, to be sure, are not so uncommon in vaudeville but everything has a newness in Coney Island.

"Which of these persons do you like best?" I asked the Little Chaperone-person.

"I like them all so well," she replied, "it's hard to choose any one."

It was so with me also—where they were all so nearly perfect of their kind it was difficult to find a favorite.

But finally we selected a gem—a gem who wore eyeglasses and walked the stage with the air of being in merely temporary durance vile. Also she had a look of some fine high respectable matron of a Girls' School in Massachusetts. She was stout and heavy and held her head high and triumphantly, and her eyeglasses had a long gold chain to them. This chain taken together with her ridiculous short frock, her green legs and the song that issued from her lips, made an incongruity so delicate that it seemed like to vanish momentarily. The words of the song could not be heard—even with that voice—in the general din and uproar, and seeing this dignified creation pacing up and down the stage you might have thought it the sleep-walking scene from *Macbeth*, or the court-room scene in *The Merchant of Venice*. You might have, only instinctively you didn't.

We gazed at this astonishing vision until our brains seemed paralyzed.

"Come," said the Little Chaperone-person, "that is the limit. Let us leave Coney Island."

So we left Coney Island—a lovable unconscious pathetic thing—and departed into the night.

But as we went we turned, like Lot's wife, and looked back.

We saw a swift picture of the beach in the afternoon; the sweet common world-old faces of happy children; the lovely eyes of little Gertrude in the sand; the very young babies and the tired work-worn mothers; the salt air from the water, and the water itself in long, long palish-blue waves and lines; the sweep and curl of white foam; the gray shadows on the sky; the dull heavy sun looking through mists; the flying wild clouds—and then a deserted beach in the dusk with water silently moving and vague mysterious phantoms coming up out of the sea.

"Everything," responded the Little Chaperone-person, sleepily.

New York Sunday World, 31 August 1902

I, MARY MacLANE

A DIARY OF HUMAN DAYS

BY

MARY MacLANE

AUTHOR OF "THE STORY OF MARY MACLANE"

NEW YORK

FREDERICK A. STOKES COMPANY

PUBLISHERS

The original title-page, 1917 (reduced)

A DAY IN WALL STREET

I have been a day in Wall Street.

To one who is in Wall Street day after day it doubtless is something peculiarly of now. To one who stands without the whirl an age-worn line of life shows plain-written upon those modern brick walls.

There is a soft monotonous ancient choir that sounds low and deep in the midst of the noise.

There is an old dull gray shadow that shows pale yet marked in the midst of glaring tones.

There is the spirit of an old, old fashion that is as old, older than far than the avarice of the money-changers in the temple.

There are human beings grasping, straining madly after treasure, each for himself.

* * *

Inside the Stock Exchange the stream of money goes its way. Men shout with lungs of leather, and their mouths and eyes are strained. The atmosphere of this building is of a greenish-grayish and copper-colored hue, and if one is standing aside and looking one imagines it plainly enough.

The men who are shouting are surely thinking of nothing but the shouting. My mind stops and marvels at this. My own mind wanders at will to the times of the Crusades, to the Ptolemys in Egypt, to Darius, to the Philistines, and to the far countries. But here are minds that stay all day long, all year long between four high narrow walls. And they are minds that go wild at times in that tiny space, in agony of suspense and anxiety for paltry reasons enough, that are aching in unrest which is more than pitiful in its utter unconsciousness.

These minds are they that mourn. Whether or not they reach their desire—whether they grow rich or poor—they are among the most unfortunate ones of Earth. They mourn, mourn, mourn always and unconsciously for what is not theirs—each over his condition in life, over the money of his fellows, over the real want of anything vital in his life. For there is nothing that is vital in all this straining.

* * *

These buildings are peculiarly places of men. There are no

feminine elements, no feminine colorings, no feminine hands. Everything is abrupt and unyielding and masculine. One can be sure, as one contemplates them, that these men have no thought of women in this mad whirling. There is no far faint echo of that soft tale within the gray high walls. To be sure, there are but few large human ways of living, such as this, in the world where there is no looking of man to woman. It is one of many outside elements lacking in Wall Street. It is well doubtless that it is lacking. All desires are distorted there—and so that also, were it present.

One knows as little as possible about the buying and selling in the Stock Exchange, or the varying condition of the money market, or the going up or going down of stocks, or the panics, or indeed any of it. But to look at it from afar it seems utterly absurd. It is obviously one-sided and the profits are so surely with the middleman. And yet men have no greater pleasure in life than to risk their fortunes in this bottomless pit. And the brokers seemingly ask no greater pleasure than to gratify them. It is one of those mills of the gods that are said to grind slowly but exceeding fine.

The great mournful spirit of unrest has come and made this her abiding-place. She lays her cold hand upon the eyes of these men and brushes their forms with her somber gray garments as she walks. She leaves nought but rage and woe behind her in her path, and the hearts that she touches are heavy. And men thereafter know not one moment's peace. A tragic vision looms before one's eyes as this thought comes—a vision of two things: one of the wondrous fair green Earth, of rapid rushings of water, of the bend of weeping willows, of the white necks of swans upon a lake, of a steep hillside, of the green bay-tree that flourisheth, and of the balm-o'-gilead; and another and present vision of minds that have wandered far from truth, that are passing by the real things, that seem fallen and lost, that are fighting, struggling, raging in a torrid glare of greenish lights in the company of ghoulish phantoms, that have forgotten the first old lessons, and go on and on with deaf ears and blinded eyes, and hearts eternally bowed down. The more so that they are unconscious and even imagine themselves content.

The life of the street, equally mad as it is, is preferable to the inside of the buildings. The street seethes with life. I have never seen so many different kinds of men as I saw during my day in Wall Street. There were men who knew values, and there were men who didn't know anything. There were men with murder in their eyes, and men with fair good-tempered faces. There were men in white duck, and men in clerical cloth, and men in unquiet plaids, and men in nondescript clothes, and men in rags, and men in shabby-genteel garments—and a fruit-vendor on the curb in a dubious red jacket and waistcoat, with brass rings in his ears. And there were as many young boys plying various extremely small trades—mostly selling the newspapers, but there was also the festive boot-black, and the vendor of shoe-strings, and the dealer in pies and gumdrops. And there was a morose individual who displayed fascinating little mechanical toys on the pavement—a strange contrast to the mighty tide of Wall Street.

The cobblestones of Wall Street have also a voice of their own. They say: "We lie under the feet of the men. We are infinitely wiser than they are. We have been here many more years than have passed over their heads. Their gigantic choruses of still voices sometimes cry out together in unanalyzed misery: 'My God, why hast thou forsaken me?' But we lie here strong and content. We do not cry; we do not rave; we do not moan. Our name is Strength-and-Patience. We are merely waiting for the end."

Ah yes—a strong, strong voice comes up from the dark gray cobblestones, a strong and somehow hateful voice. But it sounds most true.

Often, often in this long journeying, it is the hateful thing that is true.

At high noon the sun shines heavy and hot upon Wall Street and all that therein is. The faces of the tall buildings appear all threatening in the thick air, and the faces and voices of the people are heated to the cracking point. The hoarse yelling of the curb-brokers becomes hoarser and louder. The newsboys frantically cry their papers in the harsh voices of their kind. The shoestring dealers become agonizingly persistent with their line of goods, which certainly at high noon seem somewhat a drug on the market. The gumdrop-vendor gazes in heated despair at his melting delicacies but increases his efforts to dispose of them. The morose individual with his gaily-colored little toys winds them up and sets them going with twofold velocity until they seem to dance before one's eyes like motes and beams in mid-air. The fruit man in dingy red garments and the brass earrings regards his goods with extreme solicitude and raises a pathetic discordant voice in praise of them.

The entire boiling mass of humanity surges and sweeps in every direction, and pushes and jostles and becomes profane. It is an inevitable rule that all must hate each other in a crowd on a hot day, and this seemed particularly evident in Wall Street. Torrid as it was the look in some of the faces expressed, plainly, desires to see some other faces in yet warmer climes—and different kinds of hatred radiated from eyes and fingertips.

One's brain seems to ferment in that atmosphere. One thinks vaguely to one's self that hell and damnation must be like this. One looks at the buildings and the cobblestones and the people and one wonders if these are things of the moment or things of all time. Then one is sure that they are things only of the moment—that one, with one's own eyes, can see them all passing, passing, passing in one long dead march to their damp black graves.

* * *

The men move and mourn with their minds of unrest.

The high gray walls stand always, passionless, baffling—and the cobblestones.

The spire of Trinity rises high in the direction of the stars.

New York Sunday World, 7 September 1902 (abridged)

Originally titled: "Mary MacLane on Wall Street"

ON FASHION

Let the fashions be what they will, there's always a fascination in clothes. They reflect not only the follies and fads, the trend of thought, even in a qualified degree the literature and art of their day. They reflect, too, the make and manner and moods of their own wearers in a way at once subtle and illuminating.

It's as if fashion worked in its own despite. We all simply have got to follow the fashion, of course—or else be content to enjoy a popularity commensurate with that of corpses in coffins. But fifty women clad in exactly the same, perhaps delicately barbarous, mode of the hour, will wear it in fifty more widely differing ways, thus revealing their individualities, than if each were dressed regardless, to match her temperament, morals, character, or brains. You might have to look them over more carefully in order to recognize this fact, but you would recognize it—if your intuition is in good working trim. For, look you, if there were no such thing as Fashion, with a big F, and we were each allowed to choose our own style, most of us would studiously affect clothes which would conceal as nearly as possible the trend of our minds. It's the tendency of human nature to try to appear what it is not.

The grande dame wishes to give an impression of simplicity of philosophy and life. The dairy maid inclines to the sheet-iron corset and amber velvet school of thought. The fat shopwoman would fain show herself a poetry sylph in, say, a hand-embroidered Chinese coat. The so-called immoral woman of leathern conscience would dress in a way to convince the world that she is "all heart"—white India muslin with snowdrops at her breast. The literary woman, as a rule, would wear the panoply of the chorus girl. The chorus girl with—who knows?—a secret sight of relief, would don a frumpy blouse and a lopsided suit and a facial expression of sanity and sense. The fourteen-year-old girl would wear anything which seemed to her sufficiently unwieldy to feel grown up. Her revolutionary, youth-pursuing grandmother would climb into a harem suit.

Absinthe-drinking young women artists and literati would wear the schoolgirlishest of serge skirts and middy blouses, with fillets of pallid ribbon round their devoted heads. Thus it would run. We would each have our bluff to put up, and unconsciously, we would each mentally "call" our neighbor's bluff. But—we would deceive uncounted legions of men.

But with a single prevailing fashion for all of us we willy-nilly reveal ourselves. Night brings out the stars, as any high school senior will tell you. Since we must all dress alike, it devolves upon us to assert our individual style at least to the extent of wearing our gay garments different from—and better than—everybody else. And in asserting ourselves we reveal ourselves.

In other words, a shop girl, if she makes a "noise" in the way of clothes, can only make a noise like a shop girl—be her modish, million-times-duplicated frock ever so skin tight. But in clothes of her own planning and designing as to line and texture and color, who shall say that she couldn't make, in the busy marts of men, a sound like a naiad, a Chinese band, a vision of Théophile Gautier, all in one? Who shall say she wouldn't be number one, class A, in delicate incongruities?

No, let nobody run away with the idea that clothes are unimportant, or a trivial factor.

Still, and after all, what's the use? We are completely at the mercy of the man milliners. With a blind and absolute submissiveness we wear whatever they plan, and sally forth in it like lambs to the slaughter, though it work our undoing. And even now they may be planning monstrosities, whether of wigs and farthingales are but trifling adjuncts, to pay for having arrayed us like goddesses in the summer and fall of Nineteen Eleven.

Chicago Tribune, September 10, 1911 (abridged)

Originally titled: "Mary MacLane Says"

ON WOMAN SUFFRAGE

I believe in sanity and justice, and I believe in honor and integrity of women—my experience has been that they're of far more dependable and less hysterical quality than men—and these United States sadly need such things in their bodies politic.

Most men are by nature grafters and parasites. Some women are, not by nature but by training and influence of environment, grafters and parasites. But most women, when they do turn themselves inside out in the sight of the world, reveal an independence of viewpoint, and a freedom and a bravery of soul that cannot possibly be bought for money.

What I most admire about the suffragists of forty years ago and now, is their willingness to suffer for their cause. It is a rare trait in this, the day of the fourflusher. If the cause of woman suffrage had not in itself one merit, or one tottering leg to stand on, or was the tenet of fools, it still would be a fine thing and a poetic thing for the heroic sincerity that gave it birth, and that keeps it living, and that finally will triumph.

To show my belief in such women as Susan Anthony, a hero and a martyr if ever there was one, I enthusiastically and gladly would go in sackcloth. Woman suffrage never before had, and belike never will have again, another such woman for a leader. It's alas! at this restless and crucial near-crisis of it, that she is deep in her quiet grave. Still, her soul, like John Brown's, goes marching on. It stands for strength, nobility and truth.

These things by themselves hold their own and inevitably win out—and to a person like me, whose life is made up of the picturesque romanticnesses, the fascinating treacheries, the exquisitely cruel slips 'twixt the cup and the lip, the iridescent trivialities—to such as me they have their own deep compelling and enthralling charm.

I believe the most fascinating quality of the human mind and the rarest, when all's said, is sincerity—and next after that enthusiasm, that thing of fire and passion which, when given leeway, bide the sleeping soul awake in its dankest clay that breathes.

It's by those two things that the suffragists of forty years ago blazed the trail for those of the present day. Susan Anthony, gently bred and frail of body, went undaunted, sans fear and sans reproach, to a villainous county jail to live for months, amid a mixed company of prostitutes and drug-tainted women, rather than pay the fine, or let her friends pay it, which was the alternative penalty for her "improper use of the ballot": the casting of her vote for president.

The speeches of Mrs Stanton on the floor of the senate, as literature, as the expression of a high wrought, deep fired mind, and as logical argument for her cause, were recorded among the big things that were heard there, and are so recorded yet. That not-too-sane, but entirely picturesque and delightful woman, Victoria Woodhull, and her almost as picturesque sister, Tennessee Claflin, in the heyday of their youth, of their insolent beauty and good looks, and of their brilliant mentalities, turned their young energies into the channel of the suffrage movement with all the ardor of their hearts, and lent to a somber and half-lost cause a parti-colored impetus.

If woman suffrage is not likely ever to have another advocate so strong, so loyal and so noble-minded as Susan Anthony, it is equally unlikely to have one so picturesque, so valiant, so absolutely "game" as the handsome young Woodhull woman of the veiled star eyes and the goddess brow. She followed up all her enthusiasms with a headstrong belief in their rightness and justness, and a scornful regardlessness of the cost to herself, which would make in a day twenty thousand friends for the cause and twenty thousand foes for her. She made countless mistakes, but the honor of her intent redeemed them all.

The eloquence of Elizabeth Stanton and Julia Howe, and the example of Susan Anthony and Lucy Stone, meant the enrollment in the ranks of all women whom they reached. But only Victoria Woodhull—though, too, well worshipped by women—ever succeeded, on her lecture platform and of it, in hammering the cold iron of masculine indifference into malleable conversion. She brought every gift and talent and advantage she owned into the woman suffrage game—she knew its need. Her life, set as it was in New York (then as now a city of treacherous delights), might have been one of beflowered gaiety. But she cast her lot with the reformers of her day and found in it, as she made it for others, a toil and a task more enthralling, by reason at once of its humanness and its truth, than even the world-old pursuit of the flying pleasure. She likewise went to jail in punishment for some of her zeal.

All those are of a bygone era, but the history of their efforts is the most informing and convincing that the cause has yet shown. There is a splendid desolation about them in their battle for what they knew was, and would be while they lived, a hopeless cause.

Having got all of that out of my system, as they say on the "vodeville" stage, I feel free to put forth my own private and erratic brand of views anent the subject. Much and sincerely as I admire and feel inspired by the Woodhulls, and the Ida Harpers, and the Carrie Chapman Catts, and the Mrs Pankhursts, and the militant suffragettes in England, as a heroic cult, and much as I'm interested in the cause itself, I—M. MacLane—personally would be an extremely unfit person to hold a ballot.

And I am so well aware of the fact that I never would bother to vote, though all my sisters-in-arms were going, loaded and primed, to the polls. I am governed only by my impulses and affections and led on by the fascinations with which life for me is always rife. And I should cast a vote on the same picturesque principles, if I cast one at all, with no regard for such tiresome things as safe, sane conservatism.

No, when it comes to voting for president, I shouldn't be there—I should find more interest in sitting at home and mending me a pair of blue silk stockings, the while going over in my mind the affairs of the heart I might then be engaged in. I don't much believe in presidents, anyway. They don't seem to change anything, benefit anything, or "start" anything. Patent medicines with wood alcohol in them are still being sold to the public, and children are still working in the mills and mines. Trusts and combines are yet solid with themselves and the hookworm remains rampant and triumphant. So, what's the use?

We need more patriotism and fewer presidents. Until we get it, which, certes, will be quite some time, I, for one, am not going to be much interested in the politics of this domain. I am a deal keener for prizefighting—I am strong for the virile heroes of the ring.

But I am still stronger for the qualities of sincerity and

enthusiasm—which brings me back to the suffragists and my deep belief in them. The wide, long, ancient curse upon women includes limitless waiting and limitless durance and an infinite hoping against hope. They will win out, beyond a doubt's shadow, in a dozen or fourteen years, or less.

And when women do get the franchise, their work and their battling will have just begun.

Chicago Tribune, September 10, 1911 (abridged)

Originally titled: "Mary MacLane Believes in Woman's Suffrage, But She Never Could Vote for a Fat President."

Mary MacLane at the Essanay Film Studio, Chicago, 1917

MARY MACLANE AND THE MOVIES

INTRODUCTION

The critical literature on Mary MacLane's brief but memorable film career is small in quantity and weak in quality. Only a few contemporary reviewers, most notably James McQuade in *Motion Picture World*, found real merit in MacLane's acting ability in her one film, *Men Who Have Made Love to Me* (Essanay, 1918), or in the film itself. Most critics were condescending, if not outright hostile. The *Chicago Tribune*'s Mae Tinee wrote that MacLane on the silver screen "looks and acts like a headache," while the *Chicago Herald*'s Louella Parsons complained that her acting consisted of little more than smoking, swearing and drinking.

As for scholarly criticism, it scarcely exists, for neither MacLane's script for the film, nor a print of the film itself, seem to have survived.

MacLane's involvement in cinema nonetheless remains an important part of her life and work. She was not only a writer of books but also a writer of at least one film script, as well as a movie actress. How many writers are listed in *Who's Who in America* as MacLane was, as "author" *and* as "feature star in motion pictures"?

The two texts reprinted here are indispensable for an understanding of MacLane's relation to cinema: first, her 1910 article, on which the film was based (reviews make it clear that the film closely followed the article), and second, what seems to be her only article on film, in which she reflects on her own experience as an enthusiastic movie-watcher, and touches on her debut as a film actress in Chicago's Essanay Studios.

These articles do not appear to have been reprinted anywhere until now.

P.R.

MEN WHO HAVE MADE LOVE TO ME

This article is going to be very egotistical and MacLanesque and maybe somewhat shocking besides, so I strongly advise divers citizens of Butte not to read it. It occurs to me that some of the things I write do not agree with the constitutions of the said citizens—it seems to be bad for their livers—hence this preliminary note of warning. So now if you go right on and read it and it effects your liver unpleasantly, don't blame me.

To the others I fain would say this, that I aim not to instruct in these articles, neither do I aim to better people's morals, nor in fact to bore people in any other way. My aim is to write something to entertain who pay a nickel-a-throw for the Sunday News—to entertain them in the vaudeville way, artistically if I can, but, anyway, cheerfully, gayly, after the drive-dull-care-away method. If only the citizens of Butte would regard me as vaudeville and read me with a patter and kettle-drum chorus, only to be entertained! But no, the stuff comes out on Sunday and so they read it at breakfast and assuage their consciences for not going to church by knocking it and me.

And they call me a menace. All right—I'll be a menace, and if they don't look out I'll be "some menace." But at that I'll be a gay menace, a menace bound in red and gold, a menace with its hair in little curls, a menace with bells on, a menace *de luxe*. Perhaps I'll come out as the original menace. I'll hit up the menacing business in Butte—I'll let my friends in cheap at the bottom—and we'll all go a-menacing together. It'll be quite fine and dandy. And all owing to the nifty parties who read my stuff at or after their Sunday morning breakfast and don't go to church.

I am herewith going to make a few genre pictures of men I have known and loved. I would rather write about women because men are so nearly all alike and are such conventional masculine beasts, anyway. But the editor of this neat sheet said men for this article (it'll be women in another one)—so what can a poor girl do?

Since the Spring of 1902, that lucky time when I ceased to be I and became M. MacLane and left little old Butte to go and fathom the mysteries that lie along the Atlantic seaboard in the depths of cities, when I knew completely nothing about the element masculine—since that time I have met upwards of a thousand men. The women at first fought shy of me for the most part, but the men came and went in my life in a never-ending stream, like a long glittering galaxy of little gods. So I know quite a lot about them. I sha'n't write everything I know—'twould hardly bear it—but from the thronged memories within me I'll cull a few types—like as: the Callow Youth, the Literary Man, the Bank Clerk, the Prize-Fighter, the Absinthe Drinker, the Middle-Aged Gambler, the Younger Son and the Husband of Another.

If all these types seem to make love to me don't be surprised or alarmed. It's the only reason I happen to know anything about them, and besides, men always make love to women—always.

The Callow Youth

I knew him first in St Augustine Florida, where I used to spend my winters. St Augustine is a be-palmed and be-poinsettiaed winter resort of wonderful hotels, small in territory and congested in visiting population. One meets a motley moneyed company there—people from darkest Pittsburgh and deepest Indiana. And into my life one winter there blew a Callow Youth, aged but twenty; I being twenty-four. He was not only callow, but was a gilded sort of youth as well, a golden lad. His hair was the color of benedictine, his outlook on life was assured and mostly sanguine, and he looked a dream in white duck without a hat and with his sleeves rolled up over his bronzed biceps. He had a doting mother and an acrid spinster cousin, by way of family, in Stamford, Connecticut, and he himself was a Yale sophomore. But at the time I met him he was out of that institution on an involuntary vacation, the sole information he gave me on the subject being, "Poor mamma! she doesn't know I'm down here. You see it would worry her—and so needlessly—to know I'd got suspended just for wrecking a fire-engine." He had absolutely no sense of humor—his type never has, and the lack is either quite fatal or else the most delicious thing in the world. 'Twas the latter in the case of the Callow Youth—his callow name was Gerald—he took himself and all the world with a seriousness that was colossal, and for some mysterious reason he fancied himself in love with me. And for the time—and *pour passer le temps*—it was not difficult to imagine myself in love with him. He and I used to amble together at sunset when the bells in the ancient cathedral sent languid chimes out over the sea and the low waves splashed the sea wall at noon-tide, and the sky was of opals and amethysts. And thus the Callow Youth: "You know, Mary, you're the only woman I've ever known who understood me at all, and you don't know how much it means to a man. You see, a man's got to have sympathy from some woman or nothing's worth while. There are plenty who'll tell you they love you, without really being sympathetic—like poor Fluff, for instance." ("Poor Fluff" was a personage with intensely yellow hair, by surname O'Rourke, who had supported Trixie Friganza in the chorus of *The American Idea.*) "Fluff was an uncommon girl in every way, and an awfully good sort, but she always wanted so much sympathy herself, you know—it made it awkward. Now, you're so different. There's just one woman in all the world for me, from now on. Everything and everybody are dead set against me, except you, and if you should fail me now there'd be nothing before me but the grave."

At which point I always looked away at the line of opals and amethysts, whereupon he glanced at me with, "You may not even yet quite comprehend me, Mary—you may think I'm young and all that rot, but I tell you, truly and really, I'm a devil of a fellow when I get started." Alack, that he never did get "started," whatever that may mean. 'Twas full three weeks before he bored me.

The Literary Man

A type that is rife in New York town, and quite the coldest, hardest, brutalest of all who walk its busy marts, but with a certain scourge-like charm of its own—he was my *bête noir* for a matter of months. I was not happy with him nor away from him. He possessed that pleasant faculty of keeping me in a chronic state of tolerable misery. And this his manner of speech the while he sat in my little den smoking up my cigarettes and damaging sundry of my little belongings—pictures or pillows or articles of *vertu*—by roughly handling them as he talked: "Mary—Mary, you're such an incomparable idiot! I've known you long enough by this time to cease to expect even ordinary decency and propriety from that twisted concoction you call your personality—but up to now I have given you credit for ordinary intelligence. The things that I impressed upon you as distinctly not to be said, at that tea-fight yesterday, were the very things you said, and now see what's come of it—you utter fool! You have cost me just six useful friends merely by sheer wanton recklessness. I wonder if there can ever be such a thing as keeping a tab on your insanity and reckoning on it, or whether it will always be a little blighting curse on us both." Said I, in extreme discomfort, "That being the case, why don't we drop things right here?" On my left third finger blazed an oriental stone of deep-toned red, the outward and visible sign that the Literary Man and I had exchanged betrothal vows. The Literary Man: "Oh, I've promised myself to break it off—a hundred times. You've cost me so much in every way! But sometimes, and almost, I think possibly you're worth it. Let's go over to Mouquin's and talk it over."

We talked things over infinitely that winter, and a countless number of times—and he called me a liar, and an evil spirit, and an imp of darkness, and various other names, besides trampling rough-shod on my already battered heart. But withal it was I who finally broke it off, quietly and triumphantly, and with the pleasant feeling of knowing that it left him in a carping, dissatisfied mood, and with a set of assorted qualms which I think even yet flit, hornet-like, through his mind.

The Bank Clerk

His temperament may not be typical of bank clerks, and yet I've found it characteristic of men in those clerical positions which occupy them from eight in the morning till six in the evening, working for an employer, and leaving them thereafter time to indulge their poetic dreams. I have never known a magazine poet—and New York teems with them—who really had any romance in him. They are all much more interested in sausages and beer and poker games. But in clerks, from law-readers to bartenders, it runs like a vein of precious metal. The

Bank Clerk: a tall, slightly consumptive looking, rather ordinary looking chap of six and thirty—I recollect his eyes were set somewhat too close together—I knew him in Boston, a picturesque old town which harbored me five years, a town full of delicate incongruities and as capable, in its way, as New York of being one's undoing—and New York's indeed but five hours away from it. The Bank Clerk: he had made up his mind, years before, that when he happened upon a woman of ordinary good looks and possessed of an imagination, a soul above beer and skittles, he would straightway fall in love with her and ask the favor of her hand in marriage. Well, he happened upon me, and realizing only that I had an imagination, and not that I was also a perfect devil—he foolishly fell in love with me and asked the favor of my hand in marriage. And I—I never intended to marry him, but for a matter of eleven days my left third finger bore a glittering diamond set in between two scintillant sapphires. Because my own name was too ordinary he called me Rosemary: we walked on the Common Sunday noons and week-day evenings, in the teeth of November winds, the while he spoke: "To think that my long dream is realized and She is walking by my side! My dear—my dear, do you know how I look forward to six weeks from today? I have saved up in the last dozen years about six thousand dollars out of my fool salary—and all for my wedding journey! Though I've had none but a phantom bride—still I laid it up against the time when she'd be Living Reality and she and I would make a wedding journey together. Six weeks—think of it!—and you and I will have quitted this frozen New England for Naples—we'll have landed on the shores of fair Italy, where the skies are ever blue. Can you fancy, my Rosemary, the bay of Naples at nightfall, with an indigo sky above it, hung with stars such as Massachusetts will never know—stars like immense yellow daffodils and seeming so near that almost we might reach up with our hands and gather them—stars like golden tears from the tender eyes of some mammoth night goddess—stars that will be blooming there but for us? We'll rest on some rocky promontory between sea and sky, surrounded by the soft black silence, unbroken save for the remote voices of singing fishermen many feet below, and the low music of the orchestras in the little cafés that edge the bay. It will be a soft black world lit but with yellow daffodils, voiced but with far-off music, and melting with the nameless enchantments of only you and me and the feelings in us."

Thus the Bank Clerk, to whom I listened fascinated, for he meant it all. Yet—not for mine. If ever there's a wedding journey for me 'twill be to London, to nowhere but London, that vast mixture of Babylon, Ancient Rome and itself. As for the Bank Clerk—Boston is full of women—may he have found one, a better one—which might be, easily, and may they have had their day in fair Italy, where the skies are ever blue.

The Prize-Fighter

I met him in New York, a featherweight of local fame, with the lithe grace of a Greek disc thrower, the brows and lips of a demi-god, and the eyes and the mind of an unreflective terrier. His succinct name was Red, though his very beautiful hair was of a deep orange color, and though his clothes were well tailored, his taste in neckties was something indeed fierce. With him I have gone many a summer's day down to Coney, and many an evening to Sharkey's, or to Port Arthur or some other Chinese restaurant down the Bowery, and many a night have we danced away a half-dozen golden hours in the Third Avenue dance-halls. He was a delight to at least three-fourths of my senses—I think he gave me more unmixed pleasure on the little jaunts we took than any man I've yet known. "Kiddo," said he one evening, over a chop-suey, "you sure've got me going. There ain't another skirt on the planet. Jimmy Ryan, frien' o' mine, manager of the Idle Hour, 'e says to me the other night, 'e says, 'Just cast yer lamps over this bunch o' skirts on the floor,' 'e says, 'and pick the winner—she's yours.' But I shakes me head an' I says, 'Jimmy, I know a kiddo that's got 'em all skinned forty ways—and kiddo, that goes. You don't want me money and y'er the only skirt I ever knowed that was on the level. I was dippy about you the first time we went out to Coney, and I'm dippy about you yet. You may chuck me away any day, I know you ain't in me class—but I'd be dippy still." He himself was one square pal while I knew him, and he never failed to thrill me to my very finger-tips. I'm wondering, with qualms and regrets, if he's indeed dippy still.

Him, too, I knew in New York. He was good-looking in a pallid sort of way, a slender, tallish young man, a *dilettante* in letters and a follower—if that can be called following which bothers not even to note the direction of its leader—of an extremely indifferent, light-hearted, indolently reckless cult. I was fond of him for two reasons—that the light-hearted and reckless always makes an appeal to me, and that I felt my conscience in a perpetual state of assuagement (like the citizens of Butte at their Sunday morning breakfasts) by being myself in a state of but half-approval of his tenets. Every time I held back and took exception to his modes of thought, I reflected, "What a good sort I must be, to disapprove of this." It's a pleasant feeling.

In the Café Martin, Twenty-sixth Street and Fifth Avenue, at four o'clock, we spent a hundred afternoons, listening to the music, watching the people, desultorily talking, and looking upon the absinthe in its cold, sinister, death-colored seduction. The Drinker drank eight absinthe frappes in the hour, while I ambled through one. "To think," said I in half-sad protest, "that it's slowly killing you, that you've been slowly dying for two years and are slowly dying now!" And said he, quickly, "But, my child, what a sweet, sweet death to die! We are all dying, you know, from one cause or another—we are all, in this orchid-decked room, slowly moving toward our graves. So how much better to go with this exquisite poison in our veins, with the taste of it on our lips, and the flavor of it in our hearts! It brings us the flowers of life and the music of the spheres—it would bring them to you if you'd give way to it and take it as I do with ardor and delight. We would then slowly die together—a primrose death. It softens all the heart-breaks of life. My soul and body are dedicated to it and it, like a Green God of Misericorde, giveth me sundry good gifts in high reward. So drink, my child, drink to the primrose death."

I drank with him that spring too often, to the primrose death, but always under a protest—a protest not yet strong enough to let me refuse my one thin glass, and so much the less strong to make his number smaller. Presently an invisible grave began to yawn too near his careless feet. He was a charming thing, my Absinthe Drinker, but my friendship with him blew away in the autumn winds like the scattering of dead leaves.

The Middle-Aged Gambler

The memory of him brings me mirth. He was hard-headed and hard-hearted (except in my direction), with hard-looking iron-gray hair, and hard-looking fishy gray eyes. He had race-horses at Sheepshead and a great deal of money. I liked him because he was one more type of humanity, and it was my plan to crowd all the people and all the experiences I might in my life while I lived in New York—knowing that some day Butte, Montana, of deadly-thrall fame, would be again my portion. Besides, the Gambler was kind to me, though he was the sort of man who by nature is hard on women—hard on their souls and hearts and bodies, a flinty experience in their lives. He had a *penchant* for slim sweet feminine youth with an admixture of subtle brain, and he fancied I filled that bill. He came ever and anon to see me in my little green-and-white apartment in Twenty-seventh Street, into which he fitted with that aptness proverbially accredited to a bull in a china shop. He would glance contemptuously around at its thin lack of luxury as he walked about in it—he himself lived in apartments of *bizarre* and barbaric splendor—and would regard me with amorous compassion. "Kid," said he, "I've got to run out to Pittsburgh for a couple of days, and when I come back we must have this thing settled. I've told you before now that I'm crazy about you—and you must know that I am—I needn't go over that ground again. You can do whatever you like about me, but Kid, I'm damned if I'll go on like this. You need some one to take care of you—and you've got to agree to let me do it. I've thrown that into you *fifty* times, and I'm going to keep on throwing it into you til you agree to something. After that, whatever you want—I don't care what it is—anything in New York—just hand me the tip and I'll come through with the coin. Whatever I clean up on the ponies—but I've told you all that before. Come, Kid, be nice to me—say something kind." I liked him better than literary men, anyway.

The Younger Son

As for the others, the Younger Son and the Husband of Another—I'm supposed to hold the stage but seventeen minutes in this vaudeville stunt—so it's to dismiss them with cursory glances. The Younger Son was the younger son of a baronet in England, who had been busily engaged since the hour of his birth in doing nothing whatsoever. He wore a monocle. "But I'm frightfully interested in you, Mary," said he, "and New York's a frightfully interesting place—frightfully."

He and I wandered languidly around New York, languidly out to Brighton, languidly up to the Bronx, and languidly down to Coney. Languidly he loved and languidly he rode away. He had filled me with languid laughter while he stayed, then "languidly" I ditched him. A quaint experience was the Younger Son. He had managed to waste a shocking amount of my time—he was so frightfully classy!

The Husband of Another

The most exasperating invention known to civilized man. He railed at his wife and wept on my doorstep at four in the morning. Indeed, one never knew just when he wasn't going to burst into tears—otherwise one might have avoided those damp incidents. "If only I had met you thirteen years ago," he wailed, "the tragedy of all this might have been averted." "Thirteen years ago," said I, "I was just twelve years of age. I didn't know a tragedy from a glass of lemonade—and cared considerably less. Now kindly retreat from this, my little abode, for I've got to make a quick change and go up town for dinner." "Always hard—cold—heartless with me now," said he, gazing at me with a large, heavy, sodden and most annoying brand of reproach. "Is it because I'm married? It is! Oh, but I had I known you thirteen years ago!" and he managed to change the gay, chaste atmosphere of my little flat into a briny gloom, flavored with what may be termed the juice of forbidden fruit. The Husband of Another—I recall him now, and from this distance, without exasperation—with no feeling at all, in fact, but one of gratitude that the gods did not lead him up to me thirteen years ago.

So there were eight of the little gods. There were more.

May there be others! A fascinating, fascinating game. One's loves are so real—while they last. And thereafter—one day later—of what are they made, and where are they?

The nightingale that in the branches sing
Ah, whence, and whither flown again, who knows!

Yet—how much better to be wondering whither and whence the nightingale than to never have heard its mad trill!

Butte Evening News, 24 April 1910

A still from *Men Who Have Made Love to Me* (1918)

THE MOVIES—AND ME

Any time I write my opinions and impressions of this moving picture thing in its varied phases and components, it is not in the least as a critic who carps, but purely as an ardent film fan who eats up the whole game relishingly from soup to nuts.

Everybody knows it is not the critic who keep that multicolored ball rolling, but "us fans" who pay our fifteen cents and go in at the front door prepared to like every possible thing we see that's likeable and eat up every possible morsel of romance that slides Lillian-Gishfully across the screen.

Many a critic, if we are to credit their interesting dope sheets, has come away from a picture show sickened, nauseated to his hard heart's core by the tragic want of art, logic, continuity and all those juggled-up things to be found in the whole film idea as is.

But nothing like that ever happens to me. In the first place, I don't attend picture shows in order to get nauseated. And in the second place, I usually grow so delightfully fussed up with charm, thrill, appreciation and the general sense of human emotion and color that the demon art seems quite all out of it.

It is one of my theories that the true expression of the human equation never can be pure art, and pure logic and pure continuity. Human beings are not formed to that end—not while kaisers and cabarets still go on and beds continue to sag in the middle. And since—which is another of my theories—the cinematograph really does mirror human life as it really does daily happen, it can't possibly be pure art and pure logic and still be good moving picture stuff.

Charlie Chaplin is, in my opinion, the nearest thing to a perfect artist in the long gamut of film stars, and he is by that token a case in point: Charlie Chaplin does not in any way express any form of human life as it is lived in this present state of civilization.

He falls down flights of stairs nine times with the utmost abandon and runs around tables with surprising velocity and precision, but, strictly speaking, those things are unlikely to happen in most average households. The cook would leave too often, and besides it would wear out the rugs, and prove otherwise inconvenient.

No, the nonchalant Charles, though I hand it to him as an artist and a very good one, is not a favorite of mine. Nor is Mister Fairbanks, remarkable though he is for his ready mirth and his ability to jump over things. For, again, the following reasons: though indubitably great stuff it is not true to life. I have not yet known the host in any menage I've been in to go from room to room in leaps and bounds. It's all very intriguing to those who relish the bizarre and the highly improbable in pictures.

But for myself, I am the tamest, the least fiery, the most equable type of film fan. I like dramas where young people marry with lacy clothes, and a mob in the last few feet; romances where I can sit open-eyed and pensive, forgetful of passing time; and everydayish stories where I can watch Alice Brady walk and Robert Warwick frown and Valeska Suratt's back and Louise Glaum look balefully at her leading man.

Sometimes the mere look of a country hillside with the sunshine sparkling upon it, and leaves and grasses and wild flowers blowing in the breeze, to a gaze too long inured to farthest Butte or darkest Chicago, is plaisance and paradise enow.

Since nineteen-eleven when most of the stars who now bloom madly in electric lights were not even names and were in fact working humbly and anonymously for Biograph, the picture theater has been my main stand-by in moods of relaxation.

I spotted the lyric-looking Blanche Sweet as a coming star when I was totally unable to discover her name, so reticent was the screen in those days. And the famous Pickford was known but by her curls. And the artistic Walthall peered at the camera merely as a hard-working lead. And "legits" shied like frightened steeds at the mere mention of the films. And Theda Bara in her sleek darkling pride existed not.

I have trailed stars from their dawn to their be-limousined present. I have paid fifteen cents on several thousand afternoons in the far wilds of my native Butte in order to translate me from the somber colors of myself to the passionful prisms of life as presented by Mister Selig, Mister Fox, Mister World, Mister Essanay, Mister Blue Bird, Mister Paramount, Mister Triangle, et al. And I have never been disappointed.

There has always been something in every picture I have

ever seen, though it might be but the single expression of some warmly-sexed lips or eyes, that registered at rather more than fifteen cents' value. I maintain there is more of sheer beauty—world beauty, life beauty, human beauty—in moving pictures than in any other popular expression of everyday life. If there's much that is crude in it all as yet, there is much more that is lovely.

And speaking of Mister Essanay reminds me of the most astonishing thing that ever happened to me. Without effort, without volition, without, in short, wanting to, I—I have become a "film star."

Such is fame.

Nay, more, a vampire.

I had thought that it required a devilish lot of energy and pep and punch and stunningness to become one of those things. But not so. It requires languor and clothes and ease and loads of astonishingly yellow make-up. And a kindofa, sortofa vampish way with men. I have thought of myself, when it came to self-expression, purely and simply as a lit-ry woman.

But being gently induced to play the lead in a picturization of some of my own stuff I found I had all the requisites of the little old screen vampire.

I shall have a lot to write about the making of my picture when it is all over. But just at present my days are a wild maze of directors, camera men, extra people, heroes, sets, props, electricians, luncheon hours and tumblings out of bed at six o'clock in the morning.

And they tell me I have a screen personality.

Still I remain in my own accounting not a film actor, but a lit-ry lady. I am still deeply unused to grease paint. I may look like a vampire, but I continue to feel singularly unlike one. I am a fan and not a critic, and my secret hankering is to be an extra person, ad-lib-ing in a mob. *Voilá.*

Photoplay, January 1918

A LETTER

QUERY NO. 34:
WHAT HAS BECOME OF MARY MACLANE?

Can anyone tell me what has become of Mary MacLane, author of *The Story of Mary MacLane?* It made a great sensation when it was published in 1902. Is the author still alive?

Lawrence J. Grant, St. Paul, Minn.

"Notes and Queries," *American Mercury*, August 1925

ANSWER NO. 34

Yes, I am alive. I live in Chicago and like it. I am fond of the memory of my book of 1902, and any reference to it gives me a little thrill. I don't quite know what has become of me, but I believe I've changed remarkably little since I wrote that bit of revelation. I'm in these times more of a human being than a writer, but if I should feel again that I have something in me worth writing I'll doubtless write it. So *voilá*. I have my thrill, and Lawrence J. Grant has his answer. And that's that.

Mary MacLane

Chicago

"Notes and Queries," *American Mercury*, October 1925

CHICAGO WRITERS ON MARY MACLANE

Drawing from the *Chicago Tribune*,
10 September 1911,
accompanying the article "On Fashion"

Drawing for Clarence Darrow's review of *The Story of Mary MacLane*, *Chicago American*, 4 May 1902

Editor's Introduction
MARY MACLANE AND CHICAGO

Largely because she lived like a hermit, preferred not to give interviews, and above all avoided literary society, Mary MacLane has rarely been acknowledged as one of Chicago's great writers. Historians of the "Chicago Renaissance" have ignored her completely, and local autobiographers' reminiscences of her are rare. The early tag, "Montana's lit'ry lady," has misled readers and critics alike. Not that it is totally false: MacLane did live for quite a few years in Butte, and it was there that she wrote her first, best and most famous book, as well as her third book, published fifteen years later. I, for one, have no intention of challenging her right to the title of "Montana's Greatest Author."

But the fact remains, as soon as she could afford to leave Montana's "sand and barrenness," she left, and her reluctant trips back there appear to have made her miserable. Gertrude Atherton and others who visited Butte to inquire about MacLane found that nearly everyone there regarded the young author with nothing less than "virulent hatred."

Her Chicago connections, which no one seems to have written about, were numerous, strong and lasting. To Chicago, where *The Story of Mary MacLane* was published with great fanfare by Herbert S. Stone & Company, and where she enjoyed her first and most enthusiastic acclaim, Mary MacLane returned again and again. According to critic Tiffany Blake, MacLane had made firm plans, before writing her book, to attend the University of Chicago, but was unable to do so because of "a reverse in the family fortunes." She first visited the city in July 1902, a few weeks after the book came out. She stayed with Lucy Monroe, sister of the better-known Harriet who later became the renowned editor of *Poetry* magazine. It was to Lucy that MacLane dedicated her second book, *My Friend Annabel Lee*, which appeared here in 1903, also under the Stone & Company imprint. In 1917 she made her first and only movie, *Men Who Have Made Love to Me*, at Chicago's famous Essanay Studios.

"In Chicago," MacLane wrote (in an August 1902 article on Newport), "I happened upon a friendly gaiety, and some fine and good impressions that will last." Whether she ever wrote up her impressions of the city or of the people she met there is not known; her bibliography is still in the sketchy stage and new discoveries are constantly turning up. Biographically, too, our knowledge of MacLane is far from complete. Little is known about what she did in Chicago, the milieux she moved in, or what places she frequented. We do know that she was especially attracted to Lake Michigan, and that she spent much time strolling leisurely along its shores.

From 1902 until her death MacLane was a recurring "topic" in Chicago newspapers: in feature articles, news items, gossip columns and letters to the editor. How much writing she herself did in Chicago is not known, but in no other city did so many top-flight writers and thinkers—Clarence Darrow, Harriet Monroe, Henry Blake Fuller, and others—rally to her defense. She quickly became part of Chicago's "frame of reference," especially among the dissident intellectual community, and remained so for years. In the February 1903 issue of Charles H. Kerr's *International Socialist Review*—the leading journal of socialist thought in the U.S. at the time—"Father" Thomas J. Hagerty, the colorful defrocked priest and labor radical who, two years later, would play a major role in cofounding the Industrial Workers of the World (IWW), cited MacLane in an amusing polemic on the naivete of "Christian socialists." In 1925, W. A. Evans, M.D., of the *Chicago Tribune*, in a letter attempting to interest a New York publisher in the autobiography of Ben Reitman, local bohemian radical, gadfly and "clap doctor," described Ben as "a man who is proving more baffling than Mary MacLane."

Interestingly, MacLane was identified with Chicago even before she set foot in the city. It was fitting, a *New York Times* reviewer declared with obvious disgust, that *The Story of Mary MacLane* should have appeared in Chicago, for who else would have brought out such "trash," other than a depraved, reckless publisher in the Wild West's most fearsome metropolis?

Mary MacLane eventually made Chicago her permanent home. Except for a few months during which her whereabouts are unclear, she appears to have lived most of her last twelve years in Chicago—from the summer of 1917, when she came to the Essanay Studios to make her film, until her death in 1929.

To a 1925 inquirer in H. L. Mencken's *American Mercury* who wondered "What has become of Mary MacLane?" she replied: "I live in Chicago and like it." As the question implies, she lived here in isolation and obscurity, and as her response indicates, that's exactly what she wanted. Her earlier brushes with fame do not appear to have addicted her to permanent celebrity status. Her last years are, in fact, among the least known of her life. Sherwood Anderson in his reminiscences of the Dil Pickle Club in the 1920s recalled a speaker on the subject "Men Who Have Made Love to Me"—almost certainly MacLane. In view of her longstanding penchant for bohemians and other "characters," her presence at the city's most raucous bohemian free-speech joint in those years is not too surprising. But apart from that tantalizing snippet—plus the stray fact that she worked at an advertising agency—her Chicago activities remain unchronicled.

We know that she was in poor health during most of her last decade, and perhaps longer. She died of tuberculosis on Tuesday, 6 August 1929 at the Michigan Hotel, 5450 South Michigan Avenue, where she had lived for four years. "It's not death I fear, nor life," she had written in *I, Mary MacLane* (1917). "I horridly fear something this side of Death but outpacing Life a little: a nervousness in my Stomach—a very Muddy Street—a Lonely Hotel Room."

Her obituaries in the local papers played up not only the "seclusion" and "loneliness" of her last years, but also her poverty and status as "has-been" and outcast. One last time the *Daily News* featured her on page one: "Mary MacLane, Once Famous Novelist, Dies." "Dies Obscure" was the *Tribune* version, while the *Evening Post* droned "Dies in Secluded Room." Hearst's *Herald & Examiner* went all out: its headline ran, "Her Thousand Loves Desert Mary MacLane," and a subhead referred to her "Flowerless Casket."

The fact that her obit-writers referred to her as a "novelist," an "author of romances" and even (this from the *New York Times*) "a writer of sex stories," and that they cited her article, "Men Who Have Made Love to Me" as if it were a book, indicate that neither these hacks nor their editors were familiar with her writings. For the sexist press, MacLane's ideas, and what she actually wrote, hardly mattered at all, for she remained primarily a figure of scandal.

Also emphasized in the obits was the fact that she had lived her last years in what the *Tribune* called a "now colored neighborhood"—evidently further proof, in the *Tribune*'s view, of her tragic fall from the heights of fame and fortune. In truth there was nothing at all surprising about MacLane's place of residence, for her closest friend during those years was Harriet Williams, described in the press as "an educated Negro woman" and "an artist photographer," whose studio was located a few blocks away from the Michigan Hotel.

MacLane and Williams had met through mutual New York friends shortly after the publication of *The Story*—in the days when MacLane was "surrounded by freedom-seekers, poets, artists attracted by the vivacious frankness of her writings"—and they had remained good friends over the years. "She was my friend, and she was ill and needed me," Williams was quoted as saying. "That is why she lived where she did, to be close to me." According to the *Tribune*, Williams "used her own funds to make the writer's last days comfortable." I find something poignant and charming in the fact that MacLane, who was surely one of the twentieth century's most adamant transgressors of reactionary social conventions, spent her last years flouting this country's horrendous racial taboos.

It was Williams, assisted by Harriet Monroe, who made the arrangements for MacLane's funeral at Hurson's undertaking chapel at 1318 South Michigan. Aside from the two Harriets, and MacLane's mother, who made the trip from Butte, nothing is known of attendance at the funeral. MacLane had expressed her wish to be buried in Chicago. Her family, however, whose presence she had fled so many years before, denied her this last request. The remains of Mary MacLane were buried next to her father's in Fergus Falls, Minnesota.

The condescending, misinformed send-off MacLane received from the local press at the time of her death, and the fact that her books were out of print, scarce and until recently rarely cited, are sadly typical Chicago responses to its finest authors. Hail them briefly when they're young, forget about them for the rest of their lives, and name streets, parks and schools for them long after they're gone: That seems to be the procedure applied locally, with minor variations, to such different but characteristically Chicago authors as L. Frank Baum, Richard Wright and Nelson Algren—as well as Mary MacLane. The fact that no street, park or school has yet been named for MacLane goes to show that the way of women writers is harder, and reminds us that many other important Chicago women authors—including Alzina P. Stevens, Mary E. Marcy, Lucy Parsons, Neva Boyd and Dorothy Walton—are far from receiving even a small fraction of the recognition they deserve.

The following articles—by novelist Henry Blake Fuller, lawyer/essayist Clarence Darrow, poet/editor Harriet Monroe, and the anonymous editor of *The Chicagoan* magazine—show how deeply Mary MacLane and her books affected some of her illustrious Chicago contemporaries.

To the best of my knowledge, these reviews are reprinted here for the first time since their original publication.

P.R.

AN EXTRAORDINARY BOOK

The Story of Mary MacLane is an extraordinary book. It is a "human document" of the most salient character. The boldest will consider it daring; even those who are far from being prudes may find it shocking. While many who take the world and its doings more or less lightly will simply pronounce it "good fun."

Let us begin with a statement of plain facts. *The Story of Mary MacLane*—assuming the surface-show to tally with the substance—is told in the first person by Miss MacLane herself, and Miss MacLane is a young woman of nineteen or twenty who was born in Canada of Highland Scotch stock and who is at present a resident of Butte, Montana. Her Story consists of daily jottings made through the first three months of the year 1901, and comprise some 322 pages.

Miss MacLane is a genius. She herself tells us so upon her first page. Later on, she shades her statement by declaring that she is not a literary genius. But the qualification is unimportant. She is a genius, and we prefer to accept her without any qualification whatever.

One more point: Whatever she is, she is not "that quaint conceit—a girl." Now we have her.

Miss MacLane has heard of a Marie Bashkirtseff: "I am rather like her in many points. . . . But in most things I go beyond her. Where she is deep, I am deeper. . . . Where she had astonishing vanity and conceit, I have yet more astonishing vanity and conceit. . . . She was a genius, and still more am I a genius."

Miss MacLane's book is built up on four principal leitmotifs. These are: First, her own Self, which fills her eye and her mind to the exclusion of all other selves save one; second; the Nothingness of life as manifested in Butte, Montana; third, an unceasing and unabashed yearning for Happiness; fourth, the Devil. Upon these four motives she builds up a symphonic poem that is so intense, masterful and self-centered as to cast anything short of Isolde's Liebestod completely into the shade.

There are those to whom her composition will seem vocal rather than instrumental, and lyrical rather than symphonic. She takes these few simple phrases and puts them through the mill of fioratura with all the fluency, flexibility and abandon of a

Sembrich. And her breath never gives out.

Of her four themes the Devil is the chief; indeed, Mary MacLane and the Devil (the man-devil, she sometimes varies it) are practically the only two personnages in the book. She chants an ironical litany to the Prince of Darkness, each prayer ending with the refrain: "Kind Devil, deliver me." She asks him, if he will not fetch her happiness, then at least to give her the key to the door of the glittering, gleaming Bad Things. And finally she invites her fascinating man-devil to come to pass the time of day with her, and there ensues an hour of "passionate conversation."

She tells him that she has fallen in love with him and asks him to marry her. Her need is to be fascinated by a "strong and thorough villain." Her "wailing, waiting soul burns but with one desire: to be loved—oh, to be loved!" However, her man-devil, "softly compassionate," assures her that her new life under such conditions would be even harder than her old life in the Nothingness. She acknowledges the justness of his representations, and in point of fact her Story is no farther advanced on the last page than on the first. But an astonishing amount of startling rhetoric is let off on the way.

It is a pity that Miss MacLane's thought is so centered on herself as to permit but few references to her domestic environment, and fewer still to the town in which she dwells. For she can let herself go with fine effect when she only will. For example, she has a well-composed reverie on the Eating of an Olive, and a spirited rhapsody on Broiled Beefsteak and Onions, and a most striking prose-poem on the Family Toothbrushes in the Bathroom. Her one extended reference to the unlovely town of Butte is an etching that seems bitten in with corrosive sublimate—it stings and burns with the most vivid actuality.

Certainly her misappropriations are material ones only. Her ideas are all her own. Nobody could be more decidedly a repository of originality; nobody could possibly be less secondary and derivative. To a much slighter degree than might be looked for does she draw upon such sources as music, literature and art. References to these interests are scanty; Miss MacLane finds within herself all that she needs for her self-expression.

As a guaranty of good faith Miss MacLane gives a three-quarter length half-tone of herself in a frontispiece. And to remove all risk of being taxed with duplicity she expressly states that the bosom of her dress is stuffed out with nine cambric handkerchiefs. This is but one of the slightest of Miss MacLane's many confidences.

Henry Blake Fuller

Chicago Evening Post, 26 April 1902

Originally titled: "A Montana Bashkirtseff"

Sketch of Clarence Darrow, quoting his review of *The Story of Mary MacLane*, *Chicago American*, 4 May 1902

LITTLE SHORT OF A MIRACLE

The Story of Mary MacLane is little short of a miracle. No more marvelous book was ever born of a sensitive, precocious brain.

The cheap wits, the hack newspapermen and the stilted, prosy collegiates may write of Mary MacLane according to their own mental horizon or for the purpose of selling a sensation at so much per word, but this little nineteen-year-old girl, living among the sand and grime and smoke of Montana, is one of the world's geniuses—one of those rare beings whom caprice of fate now and then drops upon the Earth, generally in huts or cottages or out upon the moor or sands or waste-places of the world.

The world is filled with men and women who can write good poetry and prose; men and women whose diction is faultless and whose grammar is more obvious than their "style." The colleges and universities are grinding these out by the thousand every year. They enter the school with some originality and power, and before the diploma is granted originality must be destroyed and the power used only for the expression of conventional nothings in the dullest and most grammatical form.

Here and there in the long gray waste of literature is a genius with soul too big or young to curb—a Burns, a Whitman, a Bashkirtseff, a Mary MacLane—and these have the truth and the honesty and the inspiration to draw aside the veil and show us a real, living, naked human soul. And we read what these poets write—not to analyze its philosophy or to test its views of life, but we read it as we look at the blue sky, the green earth, the mountaintops, to see the faithful image of a living thing. We read these because the author has been so great or so foolish as to reveal the hopes and fears, the doubts, despairs and longings, the passions and feelings, which are a part of every being who ever lived upon the Earth, but which we in our cowardice and hypocrisy seek to hide and to deny.

Mary MacLane is a genius who was thrown out upon an unfriendly world in a forbidding place and who tells us of the thoughts and longings and desires of the penned and fettered soul.

Mary MacLane and her critics compare her to Marie

Bashkirtseff, her critics making the young Russian girl a genius and Mary MacLane a weak and senseless imitation. Mary MacLane is infinitely greater than Marie Bashkirtseff. The books of the Russian girl are a long, dreary desert, brightened here and there by marvelously green and fertile acres, but there is not a dull line in Mary MacLane's confessions. It is the most impossible of books from which to quote, for there is scarce a word that one feels can be left out.

To understand this marvel one must first know who she is. Probably her neighbors would not tell the same story of her life as she tells herself. The neighbors know nothing of the life of geniuses like her; the life is inward, and the neighbors, with their jealous souls and stunted brains, cannot and would not discern this life from what is manifest to them.

Here is the eternal cry of the aspiring soul. Mary MacLane voices your fettered ambition and mine, and we recognize her genius, for its truth is proved by our own hearts.

With no occupation in a dull Montana town, she turns, in sheer weariness, to the great source of inspiration and strength—Nature herself.

Mary MacLane sees more than the dry graveyard, the noxious weeds, the dull people and the uninteresting town. She is an artist and every day is beautiful, every landscape is picturesque, every stretch of wood or stream or forest or hill is a glorious panorama such as only the artist's eye can see and only the artist's soul can feel.

The mountains and hills and valleys and plains around Butte are an inspiration to the soul of Mary MacLane. The desert waste in the flow of the blood-red sunset transports her to a fairy land.

Mary MacLane sees the beauty of Nature; she sees, too, the sordidness and littleness, the petty hopes and hates, and the small ambitions and desires, of those among whom she lives and among whom we all must live.

Her own life, with its little cares and drudgeries, its grinding, wearing commonplaces, seems like all the rest. She has the philosophy to know that it is not the great things that kill and destroy us. The venomous annoying buzz of the mosquito and the canting hypocrite cost more of life and strength than the warrior's blow. So the daily trivialities of life weary the soul and cause disgust and pain.

It takes more than fame to satisfy Mary MacLane. Like all the rest she loves the "fleshpots of Egypt." Unlike the ordinary poet, she confides this to the public who would read her book. Herein Mary MacLane, Jean-Jacques Rousseau and a few others have been true to themselves and honest to the world, and, of course, the world that deceives and lies and pretends cannot approve.

She confesses to many lapses from the straight path. She has been vain, deceitful; she has posed and lied and stolen. However, like most others who do these things she does them within certain rules; doubtless her rule as to taking other people's property is quite as ethical as most rules under which property is "acquired."

Remarkable as are the thoughts of this young girl, still more remarkable is her style, her art. The ideas may be the bequeathment of generations long past, the experience of countless generations gone before, and to this is added the musings of an intense soul who turned from the barren outward life to the contemplation of herself. For the true artist may faithfully portray nature, as he sees all of life, or he may do still better and be still truer—portray his honest soul, all the real feelings, desires and thoughts of a weary, toiling, struggling human soul. This Mary MacLane has done, but to this she has added a wonderful art and style. In vividness, in rhythm, in its finish one is reminded most forcibly of Heine, in strength and ruggedness of Whitman.

The wonderful *Story of Mary MacLane* is the most human and pathetic that can be conceived. Every line is flesh and blood; its words are a beating heart and an intensely heated, throbbing brain.

Clarence S. Darrow

Chicago American, 4 May 1902

Original title: "Story of Mary MacLane *Little Short of Miracle, Says Darrow*"

A RECKLESS, FURIOUS CRY OF YOUTH

When a real book is born into the world one of two things happens—either a great noise or a great silence. The one is as unjust as the other. The silence is made up of neglect and misapprehension and fear; and the noise is made up of missapprehension and fear and gibes and perversions and distortions and the shams and perjuries of wounded egotism. But deep in the middle of both the noise and the silence is always a beginning of wisdom in the hearts of the few who, chancing upon the book and understanding it, pass on its message to the next age.

So it is with *The Story of Mary MacLane*. In this case the book, because of the reckless fury of its challenge, encounters the great noise. What a strange, shrill, foolish, angry, contradictory mingling of cries one hears in that noise, quite drowning out the sober, honest, loving voices that would speak for the truth of the book and the deep, deep pity of it. Today it is just a week old, yet already these are some of the cries:

"Mary MacLane is a lunatic and should be locked up."

"She is hysterical—a neurotic degenerate."

"She is coarse and sensual."

"She is fraud—she knows too much for any nineteen-year-old girl who ever breathed."

"She is a poseur—a liar of lies."

"The book is a character study written by some elderly literary gentleman with a fine style."

"The alleged Miss MacLane is a sham—she doesn't exist."

And so on with a thousand absurdities.

But in spite of them all, and ten thousand more, the book is tragically, bitterly, beautifully true. True not only of this lonely woman-child lost in her sand and barrenness, but also of many, many young daughters of Eve aroam in solitary places and waiting, longing for life.

This book is the heart cry of these futile souls, of women who have not yet found their place or who may never find it; who are finer than the people around them, with dreams beyond their world, desires that will not compromise, with spiritual intuitions and senses vividly alert. It is the cry of youth not yet at home in the world—is there any agony so poignant as that shiver of youth at its own futility, its unreality? Millions of young creatures feel that shiver at nineteen, and weep not tears of bitterness and despair. But soon the mood passes and they even forget it in joys and sorrows that make life real. Mary MacLane differs from them not in her suffering, but in her power of telling it. She gives us as no one else has done that poignant, exquisite moment of awakening when all the unused passions of life seem to surge together over the drowning soul, as though to test it or overwhelm it forever.

It is life's first tempest. In weathering it youth has need of all the anchors and shorelines—happy memories, sound training, the love and sympathy of friends. But if as a child one "used to weep silently in the night" and reach out in vain "a sunburned little hand" and a "hungry little heart"; if one has grown up into nothing but "sand and barrenness" and loneliness, then one's young soul, battling single-handed with the storm, may rage as violently as Mary MacLane, may shriek out as wildly against the conventions and cruelties of the unhelpful world. But in the end, if one is strong—and did not Ibsen say "the strongest soul is he who is most alone"?—in the end even such a rebel as Mary MacLane may conquer the storm and stress and become a great woman, full of wisdom and sweetness.

There are splendid lights of wisdom and sweetness in her outpouring already, and it might be well to look for these instead of quoting the extravagances, the perversions, of an overwrought brain. These extravagances and perversions are so natural and so harmless! All that talk about the devil, for example. What imaginative young girl, even the saintliest, has not had her time of dreaming of a bold, bad conquering hero who should adore and torture her? This girl has been called icily cold by her discerning neighbors in Butte—not the first time that a woman has been so misjudged because her fires burn deep instead of flaring on the surface. Cold, indeed! Such women have too much fire to be satisfied with the pale, dull glowing or the vapid flashing of most human hearts; and probably Mary MacLane will never find, in either devil or saint, full response to her own deep passion. Perhaps that "red, red happiness of the sunset sky"—even an hour of it—which she so pathetically longs for, is not for her. Hers may be the not uncommon tragedy of over-restrained lives: hard surfaces may have gathered over her fires; she may have lost the quick responsiveness by which shallow women win love and so easily get their happiness.

But there are other things besides the ego in this book, besides the racked and sensitive young soul which here flays and wounds itself in a mad dash from its prison. Let us consider the beauty in it, the literary miracle which has been noticed so little in all the comments.

Here is a little Montana girl born with an imagination and a style which send me back to Emily Brontë for a parallel. Where, since Emily Brontë, can we find this lightninglike intuition, and this special kind of simple, vivid, flashing English—direct, rhythmic, beautiful? Who among present-day writers can say so persuasively precisely what he means to say, whether the meaning be facile or subtle, elusive, poetic? Listen to some of her poetic phrases:

"The anemone lady."

"The glittering things that are."

"This dusty, dreary, wind-havocked waste."

"I and my sand and barrenness."

"Ferociously pitiable is the dried-up graveyard."

"And, hour after hour, as I walk, through my brain some long, long pageants march."

"Weep, world—why don't you?—for poor little Mary MacLane."

"And I am unable to judge which is the more savagely forlorn: the starved-hearted child or the the woman young and all alone."

"And she reached out with a little sunburned hand to touch and take something."

"And it had a nothingness—do you hear?—a nothingness?"

"There will always be a lacking, a wanting—some dead branches that never grow leaves."

"The young, slim age of nineteen."

"Through the life everlasting—it will be as one day; or for one day—it will be as the life everlasting."

"The choir of faint, sweet voices comes to me incessantly

out of the blue."

"That quaint conceit, a girl."

"Absurdly, grotesquely, tearlessly, sad."

"It has sharp knives in it—has nothingness."

"I hear the high, swelling, half-tired, half-hopeful song of the world."

"Some one forgot me in the giving of things."

"The anemone lady came down from her high places and wrote me two letters."

And then sometimes such deep, terrible, pentrating truth, as in this saying of pain: "If it were pain alone that one must bear, one could bear it. One could lose one's sense of everything but pain. But it is pain with other things. It is the sense of pain with the sense of beauty and the sense of the anemone. . . . It is these mingled senses that torture me."

Or this of the divinity of humor: "I have a sense of humor that partakes of the divine in life. . . . It is humor that is far too deep to admit of laughter. It is humor that makes my heart melt with a high unequaled sense of pleasure and ripple down through my body like old yellow wine. A rare tone in a person's voice, a densely wrathful expression in a pair of slate-colored eyes, a fine, fine shade of comparison and contrast between a word in a conversation and an angle-worm pattern in a calico dressing jacket—these are things that make me conscious of divine emotion."

I should like to quote the entire episode of the Italian peddler woman which follows here. For sheer literature I know of nothing written in recent years to equal it. It is so simply, so vitally, so beautifully done; and through the everyday little incidents are given so brilliantly the infinite lights. I like Mary MacLane best in chapters like this or the description of Butte, where she forgets herself, and in them I find the most promise of the great artist we hope for in her. Such places are rare in this book, because her life thus far has looked outward so little. But meantime she gives us such a picture as has scarcely before been painted of the variability of the human soul of the action and reaction upon it of nature, people, things.

Each of us knows that he is a thousand different and even contradictory creatures. but who has made real the metamorphoses like this brave little Montana girl? She eats an olive—how delicious is this epicurean chapter!—and straightway "the fair Earth seems to resolve itself into a thing oval and crisp and good and green and deliciously salt." And those toothbrushes—who has not shrinked with her at the perversity of things inanimate? And the way happy nature has of making over the soul, and also cruel nature, and the January wind, and the gray dawn, and the red, red sunset sky; and sudden blessed friendship, with its "snapping of tense-drawn cords, its strange new pain"—these chapters are all of them exquisitely wrought, which sing nonetheless musically for being in prose.

Yes, Mary MacLane is a poet—a point which, I think, none of the critics have mentioned. There are splendid sounds and harmonies in her thrilling vibratory prose, and to me the most wonderful thing in her wonderful book is her use of the refrain. Nowhere, save in her own soul, could she have learned this incommunicable secret of returning at exactly the right moment to the keynote, the telling, insistent, echoing phrase. Over and over she repeats her beautiful phrase, yet never once too often, never once too little. And thus some of her chapters are fine harmonies, as rhythmic, as resonant as a sonata, as definite in form and climax.

Ah, me! I had a number of other things to talk about today, but who can turn from this imperious book or say half that he wants to about it?

Harriet Monroe

Chicago American, 10 May 1902

Original title: "More About Mary MacLane's Book"

UNQUENCHABLE FIRES

Butte, Montana, returns to the map; Mary MacLane has written another book.

"Is it like the first?" you will ask. It is. "Is it as good—or as bad?" It is.

It is also named nearer to the heart's desire of the author. *The Story of Mary MacLane*, dating some twelve years back, had its title imposed from without. But *I, Mary MacLane*, the book of today, has surely been named from within.

One to whom editorial chance gave the opportunity of making public the first picture and the first biographical sketch of Butte's egoistic young sybil could scarcely remain indifferent to her latest fluttering of leaves; old associations must be allowed to count.

The new book, like the other, consists of a series of set-pieces strewn over a palpitating field of passional protoplasm—just as king-crabs and quahaugs and jellyfish and other odd forms of life are strewn over the tide-bared mudflats of Long Island. The palpitant protoplasm, being constant, may be taken for granted; so one naturally fixes his attention on the set-pieces. Such things as ornamented the other books—things like "I Await the Devil's Coming," the famous "Litany," and the "Gray Dawn"—are duly succeeded by similar creations, such as the "Cold Boiled Potato," the "Helliad," the rhapsody on Keats, and the extraordinarily ingenious, fantastic, poignant chapter on the visits of "My Soul." The best of these *jeux d'artifice* show unmistakably the gains of experience and in skill made during the intervening years; they are rather better in themselves and rather better adjusted to their background. Yes, the web now spun by the Arachne of the Copper Hills is somewhat finer than the first one, and somewhat more delicate—even when indelicate.

As for the Mary MacLane of 1917, she is essentially the same creature as in 1905. The comet has returned, after many years in the dark void, with as much incandescence and momentum as ever. In a chronological review of the many Mary MacLanes—for "Introspection" has wrapped our adventurer in a "Winding Sheet"—we are told through what spaces the comet has journeyed during these years (and others), and we learn something of the various bodies—not always celestial—past which it has hurtled.

And today the skyey voyager sits "here this midnight in a neat blue chair in this Butte, Montana," with all the old hamperings still holding and all the old hankerings still unappeased, and pauses to consider her own representative quality. She is conscious of a legion of women of the same "psychic breed," who "may be sitting lonely in neat red or neat blue or neat gray or neat any-colored chairs," in Wichita, or South Bend, or Waco, or La Crosse, or in some other of many places, "each waiting, waiting always—waiting all her life—not hopeful and passionate like Eighteen, but patient or blasphemous or scornful or volcanic like Early-Thirty: . . . each more or less roundly hating" her Waco or Wichita, or whatever other place, "and each beset by hot unquiet humannesses inside her and an old yearn of sex and the blood warring with myriad minute tenets dating from civilization's dawn-times."

One may read the newer Mary MacLane and feel, after all these years—save for a touch of impatience over a problem that remains static—but little change of sentiment toward her. One is conscious, as before, of an admiring wonder at the power of her untameable and unclassifiable "call" to write, and at the amazing fashion in which, as a unique source of primary energy, she spins literature out of her very inner self; and one retains (whether impatience supervenes or no) a disposition, while viewing the temerarious disclosures of this very special soul, to be a little tender and a little sorry. But perhaps Mary MacLane, world-weary and world-hardened, would not greatly thank one for either.

Henry Blake Fuller

The Dial, 3 May 1917

MARY MACLANE: FIRE OF YOUTH

Some years ago—twelve or thirteen—a weird witch-light descended out of the air upon me in the person of Miss Mary MacLane. Anything more quaint and subversive—wise in deep ways, absurd in odd vanities, both quiet and volcanic, with a mind that undermined into dark corners and shook its little torch at the sun itself—I never expect to see in human flesh than this young and pretty girl from Butte, Montana.

She had written a book of wild youthful revolt, a book which made a noise even though it had a streak of genius in it. The noise subsided, and the maker of it has not again interrupted the silence until now. The new book, *I, Mary MacLane*, is once more introspective, but more mature (though still absurdly young in spots) and less rebellious. It is not poetry, but one may step out of *Poetry*'s province to say a word for its prose, which rises at times to heights of pure beauty and bright imaginative intensity. Of an odd and whimsical, or even tragical, humor of laughter in such chapters as the one on Lot's wife or the Finn woman, it becomes in others—those on Keats, or her dream child, or the voices of children—poignantly wistful, sorrowful with the sorrows of the world.

There are absurdities, no doubt—moments of world-obliterating egotism which fail to convince. But on the whole one gets an impression of piercing sincerity and strange beauty, at times of poetic and luminous vision.

Harriet Monroe

Poetry, June 1917

A REVOLUTION IN MANNERS

The death of Mary MacLane, a friendless recluse in an obscure hotel-room on the southern fringe of Chicago's Black Belt, evoked some excellent sob-writing. Once more, after years of shabby oblivion, she rated as first-page stuff. And now that the last chapter of her frantic life has been written; now that she has gone back with eternally stilled lips to the home-town from which she fled with printed shrieks of rebellion, her case should be referred to a higher court than the press. The social philosophers would do well to consider Mary MacLane in her historical significance.

This errant daughter of literature, whose collected writings might easily be given the title *Memoirs of My Libido*, was the first of the self-expressionists, and also the first of the flappers. She represented the missing link between the shaved bare leg of the present and the bashful ankle of the past. She should be as important to the student of modern manners as the Java ape-man is to anthropologists. She throws the subject into perspective, for she broke loose upon a startled world as far back as 1902. The modern girl's delight in shocking her ancestors and strutting her sex is as old as the first edition of *The Story of Mary MacLane*.

How did it happen that a revolution in manners, a transvaluation of values in the female code of behavior, started, or seemed to start, with an unruly young woman who couldn't bear the sight of the toothbrushes hanging up in the family bathroom at Butte, Montana? What seed fell upon that austere provincial soil to produce this amorous diarist with a narcissus complex? What mystic or glandular voices spoke to Mary, bidding her go forth into the world as the Jeanne d'Arc of the Warm Mamas?

The New Woman has had many famous prophets, from Susan B. Anthony to Henrik Ibsen. But the origin of her wild young sister, the New Female, has not yet been carefully traced. The career of Mary MacLane is Chapter I in *The History of Flapperism*, ready made for any ambitious sociologist. This is a work that is crying to be written—yea, crying out loud.

The Chicagoan, 31 August 1929

Originally an untitled editorial

BIBLIOGRAPHY

I. Books by Mary MacLane

The Story of Mary MacLane. Chicago: Herbert S. Stone, 1902.

My Friend Annabel Lee. Chicago: Herbert S. Stone, 1903.

I, Mary MacLane. New York: Frederick A. Stokes, 1917.

II. Secondary Sources

Anderson, Sherwood. *Memoirs.* New York: Harcourt, Brace, 1942.

Atherton, Gertrude. *Adventures of a Novelist.* New York: Liveright, 1932.

Blake, Tiffany. "Sidelights on Case of Mary MacLane." *Chicago Evening Post*, 17 May 1902.

Breton, André, and Paul Eluard. "Notes sur la poésie," in Breton, *Oeuvres complètes* I. Paris: Gallimard, 1988.

Ferlinghetti, Lawrence, and Nancy Joyce Peters. *Literary San Francisco.* San Francisco: City Lights Books and Harper & Row, 1980.

Garland, Hamlin. *Companions on the Trail.* New York: Macmillan, 1931.

Hagerty, Thomas J. "Socialism vs. Fads," in *International Socialist Review.* Chicago: Charles H. Kerr, February 1903.

"Have You Read the Story of Mary MacLane?" Advertisement in *Chicago Evening Post*, 24 May 1902.

Mattern, Carolyn J. "Mary MacLane: A Feminist Opinion," in *Montana: The Magazine of Western History*, XXVII:4, Autumn 1977.

McQuade, James. Review of *Men Who Have Made Love to Me* in *Motion Picture World*, 28 January 1918.

Mencken, H. L. "The Cult of Dunsany," *Smart Set*, July 1917.

Parsons, Louella. "On Movies" [review of *Men Who Have Made Love to Me*], *Chicago Herald*, 25 January 1918.

Pascoe, Peggy. Untitled research paper on Mary MacLane, 1978. Copy in possession of the Butte-Silver Bow Public Library.

Pruitt, Elisabeth, ed. *Tender Darkness: A Mary MacLane Anthology*. Belmont, California: Abernathy and Brown, 1993.

"Remarkable Book from Out of the West," *Chicago American*, 26 April 1902.

Rosemont, Penelope. Introduction to a selection of MacLane's writings in *Free Spirits: Annals of the Insurgent Imagination.* San Francisco: City Lights Books, 1983.

Spacks, Patricia Meyer. *The Female Imagination*. New York: Avon, 1975.

Tinee, Mae. Review of *Men Who Have Made Love to Me. Chicago Tribune*, 25 January 1928.

Triggs, Oscar Lovell. *The Changing Order*. Chicago: Charles H. Kerr, 1906.

Wheeler, Leslie. "Montana's Shocking Lit'ry Lady," in *Montana: The Magazine of Western History*, XXVII: 3, Summer 1977.

Wurdz, Gideon. *The Foolish Dictionary*. New York: Grosset & Dunlap, 1904.

III. Obituaries

Chicago Daily News, 7 August 1929

Chicago Evening Post, 7 August 1929

Chicago Herald & Examiner, 8 August 1929

Chicago Tribune, 8 August 1929

New York Times, 8 August 1929

A NOTE ON THE EDITOR

Born in Chicago in 1942, surrealist poet/painter/photographer Penelope Rosemont was active in the *Rebel Worker* Group (the "left wing of the Beat Generation") in the mid-1960s, and served on the National Staff of the Students for a Democratic Society (SDS) in 1967–69. In January 1966 she and her husband Franklin were welcomed by André Breton into the Surrealist Group in Paris, and later that year organized the first indigenous Surrealist Group in the U.S., in Chicago.

Rosemont has published two volumes of poems, *Athanor* and *Beware of the Ice* (the latter illustrated by Enrico Baj), and she is represented in many surrealist anthologies. As painter, collagist and photographer she took part in the first Chicago Surrealist Group show at the Gallery Bugs Bunny in 1968, and since then has participated in numerous international surrealist exhibitions—in France, England, Holland, Mexico, and other countries. At the 1976 World Surrealist Exhibition in Chicago she elaborated the Domain of Robin Hood. Her work has also been shown at the Venice Biennale.

She is a co-editor of *The Forecast Is Hot! Tracts and Other Collective Declarations of the Surrealist Movement in the United States, 1966–1976*, and has recently completed *Surrealist Women: An International Anthology*. A volume of her selected articles and essays is currently in preparation.